THE LAST WORDS
FROM THE CROSS

PRAISE FOR
THE LAST WORDS FROM THE CROSS

William Powell Tuck's, *The Last Words from the Cross*, gives this generation a fresh and tender insight into the last words of Christ from the cross. Tuck's ability to strip away many common and often wrongly held beliefs and traditions about Jesus' final words from Calvary is deeply thought-provoking. Tuck provides powerful and poignantly descriptive details into the humanity of Jesus as he processed the raw, gut-wrenching emotions of forgiveness and compassion and ultimate separation from his father.

Tuck's well researched work brings the reader to the foot of the cross as if transported in time to Christ's crucifixion. As you read, be prepared for a gamut of emotions to sweep through your heart and mind. From moments of ecstasy and joy, to those mixed with tension and profound grief, Tuck helps the reader to grasp the tremendous price that was paid on a Roman cross for humanity. Truly, Tuck has captured in a most remarkable way the essence of God's love shown through his son's last words from the cross.

D. Kevin Brown, Pastor
Mt. Pleasant Baptist Church, Wilkesboro, North Carolina
Author of *Rite of Passage for the Home and Church*

Over the years Dr. William Powell Tuck has written a number of books that have encouraged and challenged readers from a variety of backgrounds. His latest work, *The Last Words from the Cross*, though short in length, may be his finest effort. Dr. Tuck explores Jesus' final words from the cross in a devotional manner, creatively incorporating decades of pastoral experience and the best of contemporary scholarship. The result is an engaging reflection which invites the reader to ponder not simply Jesus' death but the whole of his life as well as the implications for all who seek to follow him.

Christopher Chapman, Pastor
First Baptist Church, Raleigh, North Carolina

Bill Tuck has provided us with a masterful interpretation of the 7 last words of Christ with his scholarly biblical analysis, solid theological research, and vivid illustrations. His eminently readable presentation makes the crucial issues of faith understandable and accessible for laity and clergy alike.

Tom Graves, President Emeritus
Baptist Theological Seminary at Richmond

Fast re-wind, and William Tuck takes you back 2,000 years to Golgotha to the agony and disorientation of the crucifixion of Jesus Christ. Fast forward, and he connects the meaning of the cross to our own times of confusion and angst and you experience hope and joy rising within you through his riveting stories and keen insights.

Kent Ira Groff, founding mentor of Oasis Ministries
retreat leader and author of *Clergy Table Talk*
and *Honest to God Prayer.*

OTHER BOOKS BY
WILLIAM POWELL TUCK

The Way For All Seasons

Facing Grief and Death

The Struggle For Meaning (editor)

*Knowing God: Religious Knowledge
in the Theology of John Baillie*

Our Baptist Tradition

Ministry: An Ecumenical Challenge (editor)

Getting Past the Pain: Making Sense of Life's Darkness

A Glorious Vision

The Bible As Our Guide For Spiritual Growth (editor)

*Authentic Evangelism: Sharing the Good News with Sense and
Sensitivity*

The Lord's Prayer Today

Christmas Is for the Young... Whatever Their Age

Through the Eyes of a Child

Love as a Way of Living

The Compelling Faces of Jesus

THE LAST WORDS
FROM THE CROSS

WILLIAM POWELL TUCK

Energion Publications
P.O. Box 841
Gonzalez, FL 32560

www.energionpubs.com

2013

Cover Design: Jody Neufeld

ISBN 10: 1-938434-57-9
ISBN 13: 978-1-938434-57-0

Library of Congress Control Number: 2013932755

Energion Publications
P. O. Box 841
Gonzalez, FL 32560
energionpubs.com

For the churches I have served as pastor –

Good Hope Baptist Church, Aroda, Virginia

Calvary Baptist Church, Slidell, Louisiana,

Harrisonburg Baptist Church, Harrisonburg, Virginia,

First Baptist Church, Bristol, Virginia.

St. Matthews Baptist Church, Louisville, Kentucky,

First Baptist Church, Lumberton. North Carolina

TABLE OF CONTENTS

PREFACE

John Stott reminds us that although the cross is without question the central symbol of the Christian faith today, that was not always the case. At first the early church avoided it because of its shameful association with the execution of common criminals. The symbols of the fish, peacock, a dove, or the athlete's victory palm were some of the earliest Christian motifs as seen painted on the walls and ceilings of the catacombs.[1] Today many of the so called "growing" churches or the "prosperity gospel" churches or the churches that only want positive thoughts and not signs of weakness or defeat continue to avoid any image of the cross in their buildings. But can a church be an authentic Church and not focus on the cross? Jürgen Moltmann asserts that "As far as I am concerned, the Christian church and Christian theology become relevant to the problems of the modern world only when they reveal the 'hard core' of their identity in the crucified Christ..."[2] The Apostle Paul did not hesitate to put the cross at the center of his preaching. In 1 Corinthians 1:18-31 Paul declares that some may see the cross as a "stumbling block" or "foolishness," but he proclaims it as the "wisdom and power of God." Fred Craddock thinks that the primary reason that Paul had to preach the cross was "because the cross tells us how God is. God identifies with human suffering; God comes to us and suffers with us and sympathy is extraordinarily powerful."[3]

I will never forget a course I had on the Atonement in seminary under James Tull. He made undeniably clear to me the New

1 John R. W. Stott, *The Cross of Christ* (Downers Grove, Illinois: InterVarsity Press, 1986), 20.
2 Jürgen Moltmann, *The Crucified God* (New York: Harper & Row, 1974), 3.
3 Fred B. Craddock, *The Collected Sermons of Fred B. Craddock* (Louisville: Westminster John Knox, 2011), 240.

Testament emphasis on the cross and its centrality for the Christian faith. In a book, *The Atoning Gospel,* which Tull later wrote, he stresses the fact that no one can look at the cross with discerning eyes and believe that God makes light of sin. The cross reveals with poignant, stark, all-revealing illumination and unforgettable power what God thinks and feels of our sins.[4] Can anyone fully discern Jesus' knowledge of his own impending death on a cross? Surely he did not have an advanced card describing exactly how the events of what came to be called the "Passion Week" would unfold. Whatever one says about the divinity of Jesus has to be understood in the light of his genuine humanity.

The words of our Lord on the cross have become very memorable. These words of Jesus have been designated as the seven last words. They are, of course, more than individual words. They are really sentences or fragments of sentences. One of these seven words is found in the Gospels of Matthew and Mark. Three of them are found in the Gospel of Luke, and three are recorded in John. No one gospel contains all of them. But, to me, that is a way of authenticating the gospels. Each writer drew on what he remembered or considered most important in those moments or what he had heard from others who shared their experiences.

"The cross is the surest, truest and deepest window on the very heart and character of the living and loving God," N. T. Wright declares. "The more we learn about the cross in all its historical and theological dimensions, the more we discover about the One in whose image we are made and hence about our own vocation to be the cross-bearing people."[5] The last words of Jesus on the cross reveal something about the significance of that cross event but also about how Jesus faced the event and its deeper meaning. These last seven words of Jesus on the cross give us insight into Jesus' inner thoughts in these moments of dying, a deeper understanding of

4   James E. Tull, *The Atoning Gospel* (Macon, Georgia: Mercer University Press, 1982), 59-60.
5   N. T. Wright, *The Challenge of Jesus* (Downers Grove, Illinois: InterVarsity Press, 1999), 94-95.

his suffering, and they provide us with a sense of the relevancy of our Lord's suffering to address our own needs. These words reveal his personal agony, his concern for others, his forgiving spirit, his physical suffering, his ultimate trust and faithfulness in the One he had proclaimed. Even in his moments of forsakenness he still resisted the temptation to turn away ultimately from God's will or deny the One who led him to this shameful death as he identifies with sinners. A study of the last words of Jesus on the cross can open for us, in a small way, a perspective on how Jesus met his death, but this emphasis may also instill a renewed vision of the deeper meaning and significance of the cross event – the central motif of the Christian faith. I want to express a special word of appreciation to Linda McNally for her careful proofreading of my original manuscript.

CHAPTER 1

A Prayer of Forgiveness

LUKE 23:26-34

Quietness had settled over the room. The family moved closer to the bed of the dying father. They could tell that he was trying to say something, and one of the sons in the family leaned over his father. He put his ear to his father's mouth and listened. He heard his father say with his last breath: "I love you." Then his father was gone.

Many persons have tried to capture the last words of famous, distinguished individuals or loved ones. Persons in their last few moments before they died, if they have had enough consciousness to express themselves, have sometimes spoken of seeing light, a tunnel, the presence of a loved one who had died earlier, or angels. Some have acknowledged fear or a sense of peace. Yes, we have often wanted to know what the last words were which a person said before he or she died. In the Bible, there is a record of only a few individuals whose last words are recorded before they died. These four individuals are Jacob, Moses, Stephen, the first Christian martyr, and Jesus. Our attention here focuses on the last words of Jesus.

THE JOURNEY TO THE CRUCIFIXION

Picture in your mind the background setting that led to Jesus' crucifixion. Jesus had just finished praying in the Garden of Gethsemane. He walked out of the garden and was immediately arrested by the soldiers of the high priest. He went through several mock trials before Pilate, Herod, and the high priest. He suffered the awful scourging where his flesh was literally ripped from his naked back by the whip which contained pieces of bone or iron. In his weakened condition following this scourging, Jesus was forced to bear his cross to the Place of the Skull.

While he was en route to the place of crucifixion, the crowd of people taunted him along the way and he fell under the weight of the crossbeam. A stranger, Simon of Cyrene, was forced to bear his cross to the place of execution. Mark notes that Simon's sons are Rufus and Alexander (Mark 15:21). These two men must have been known to the readers and likely had become outstanding Christians. Simon, who had met Jesus by chance on the way to his crucifixion obviously had had his life changed by that encounter. His sons were likely converted later and became such distinguished members of the early church that, when Mark writes about this experience and mentions their names, he thinks that his readers will recognize their names immediately.

Jesus finally arrived at the Place of the Skull, which stood outside the city walls. He was laid down on the crossbeam and crucified. While hanging on the cross for six hours, from nine in the morning until three o'clock in the afternoon, Jesus uttered what has come to be known as the seven last words. Let us look at each one of these words, sentences or word fragments, and see if we cannot gain some deeper insight into the cost of the suffering that Jesus endured and how you and I are affected by these words and this event. His first words, "Father, forgive them," was directed to his enemies – those who were crucifying him or who caused this event.[1]

JESUS' FIRST WORD IS A PRAYER

First, what was Jesus doing? What is this first word? Notice that Jesus' first word from the cross was a prayer. He prayed: "Father, forgive them." In his moment of suffering he prayed.

---

1   Howard Marshall, Commentary On Luke (Grand Rapids: William B. Eerdmans Co., 1978), 867 ff.

A Life of Prayer

Prayer was a natural and instinctive thing for Jesus. His whole life had been saturated in prayer. He would arise early in the morning and pray. He prayed sometimes at noon, before meals, before he selected his disciples. Sometimes all night was spent in prayer. He prayed before his temptations and at every significant moment in his life. Here in this moment of agony, he still prayed to God, because prayer was a central part of his life. Jesus' disciples had been so impressed by his prayer life that the one thing they asked him to teach them was about prayer. "Lord, teach us how to pray," they asked.

An Unselfish Prayer

Notice also that Jesus' prayer was unselfish. "Father, forgive them," he prayed. When you and I get in some difficult situation, what is usually our first response? "Oh, Lord, help me!" "Get me out of this!" "Lord, why am I here? What have I done to deserve this?" But Jesus' prayer was not for himself, but for others.

A Continuous Prayer

Note further that the prayer that Jesus uttered here was an affirmation of what he had taught. The verb "forgive" in the original Greek means that this prayer was not voiced just once but was a continual prayer.

The words, "Father, forgive them," were spoken several times. Was this the prayer that Jesus prayed when the soldiers stripped him of his garments and stretched him out on the cross and drove the nails through his hands and feet? Did he cry, "Father, forgive them" when the soldiers lifted up his cross and dropped it with a thud into its hole? Did he cry, "Father, forgive them" when the soldiers gambled for his robe? Did he pray, "Father, forgive them" when the crowd mocked him and the criminal on one side of him jeered at him from his cross? Did he pray, "Father, forgive them" when his disciples fled for fear of arrest themselves?

Jesus Lived What He Taught

This prayer was indeed a continuous prayer in the life of Christ. It reflected the kind of life that he had lived. Jesus Christ had taught others to be forgiving. "Forgive seventy times seven," he taught his disciples. Be limitless in your forgiveness. His words reveal that he practiced what he preached. When he came to the darkest moment in his life, he prayed that those who were hurting him might be forgiven. He had taught his disciples to forgive seventy times seven, to turn the other cheek, and to go the second mile.

Now in his time of testing as he was being crucified, what Jesus had taught on a mountaintop, he now displayed in his life while he was in the agony of the valley of despair. What he had taught his disciples along the bright sunny shores of the Sea of Galilee, he demonstrated was real in his words uttered in this dark moment in his life. What Jesus had taught about the universal love of God for all persons was seen reflected in his life and the way he died when he was nailed to a stake outside the Jerusalem walls by the crossroads of humanity. The Golden Rule was not merely verbiage or preaching for him, but it was demonstrated in his words in the last moments before he died. He lived the Golden Rule he taught.

An Intimate Relationship with God

This prayer also reveals the absolute intimate relationship that Jesus had with God the Father. Like a child, Jesus reached up to his Father for support in this difficult moment. He knew that the God to whom he had prayed before would still be present. The God he had known on bright sunny days was still with him on this dark dreary day. The God about whom he had taught his disciples to ask anything, he still prayed to now with assurance. He had prayed to his Father on calm days; now in the worst storm of his life, he again appealed to the One who had sustained him in the past. His trust was tested by this awful experience, but he reached out to the One whose presence was real to him. The word "Father" speaks volumes about intimacy.

FORGIVENESS FOR WHOM

Secondly, for whom was Jesus asking forgiveness by his Father? "Father, forgive them," he prayed. About whom is he speaking here?

CURSES WERE OFTEN HEARD

The executioners were not surprised that Jesus made some kind of outcry at the crucifixion. They expected any man who was led to the place of execution to make some kind of outcry. But these outcries were usually curses, jeers, and profanity. When a man faced being driven to a stake, crucified by having nails driven through his hands and feet, he would often fight and struggle with his executioners. It was a terrible experience for the person being crucified.

Cicero once wrote that the blasphemy of those being executed was sometimes so bad that the soldiers would cut out the tongue of the man being crucified to keep him from railing and screaming blasphemies. But from Jesus there were no curses, jeers, defense, condemnation or requests. He prayed simply, "Father, forgive them." His prayer, "Forgive them," reflected in his dying what he had lived and taught.

TO WHOM WAS THIS PRAYER DIRECTED?

About whom was he speaking when he uttered this prayer? Who was it? Did he pray, "Father forgive them," as the soldiers drove the nails in his hands? Was the prayer directed at the Jewish leaders, Annas and Caiaphas, the high priests or the Pharisees and the other members at the Sanhedrin who had condemned him? Were the words directed at Pilate who had washed his hands of this affair and didn't really want to get involved? Did he pray for Herod who had put a robe on Jesus and mocked him and then sent him

away? Was he praying for the crowd who had cried: "Crucify him?"
Did he pray for Judas who had betrayed him? Was his prayer for
his disciples who fled?

These words, "Father forgive them," were so disturbing to the
early church that some of the earliest manuscripts like *Codex Vat-
icanus* or *Codex Bezae* do not contain them.[2] Why? Because early
Christians didn't know how to deal with them. How could they
pray and ask forgiveness of the Jews and Romans for what they had
done? But how like Jesus these words really are. Rob Bell reminds
us that "Jesus forgives them all, without their asking for it." He
continues: "Forgiveness is unilateral. God isn't waiting for us to get
it together, to clean up, shape up, get up-God has already done it."[3]

WE ARE ALSO ACCUSED

To whom are these words directed? You and I don't get off so
easily here. These words do not point only to someone in the past.
Paul and other New Testament writers have clearly stated that all of
humanity was involved in this crucifixion. You and I, our sins, also
nailed him to that tree on Calvary. The old spiritual asks: "Were
you there when they crucified my Lord? Were you there when they
nailed him to the tree? Sometimes it causes me to tremble . . ." and
well it should! We are involved because of our sins.

You and I also need to hear the words, "Father forgive them."
They are also prayed for you and me. Unfortunately, we continue
to crucify Jesus today. Jesus, the great high priest, continues to pray
for you and me. "Father, forgive them," he implores, "they know
not what they do."

2   George Buttrick (editor) "The Gospel According to Luke," *The Interpreter's
    Bible, vol. VIII* (New York: Abingdon Press, 1952), 408.
3   Rob Bell, *Love Wins* (New York: HarperOne, 2011), 189.

WHY DID JESUS ASK GOD TO FORGIVE?

A Plea of Ignorance

Then thirdly, *why* was Jesus asking his Father to grant forgiveness to these people? He said, "Because they do not know what they are doing." This view is echoed in the New Testament. In his speech in Jerusalem, Peter said: "I know that, through ignorance you did it" (Acts 3:17). The Apostle Paul stated that Jesus was crucified because they did not know him (Acts 13:27). In another place Paul wrote: "None of the rulers of this age understood this; for if they had, they would not have crucified the Lord of glory" (I Cor. 2:8). In the parable of the judgment Jesus notes that those who stand before the Lord will plead ignorance. "When did we see you hungry or thirsty . . . or naked . . . or in prison?" Jesus responds by saying: "As you did it not to one of the least of these, you did it not to me" (Matt. 25:3146).

Not Sentimentality

Well, is this just a sentimental statement from Jesus? "Oh, it doesn't make any difference, God. It's o.k. to let them crucify me." Obviously, that is not true. His words do not mean that he is praying to let bygones be bygones. He is not saying that it doesn't make any difference to God. It does. God will not wink at this act and say, "It is OK." Of course not!

Too often we blame circumstances for what we do. Or we blame heredity and try to put the burden on our parents' back. We blame our education or the lack of it. Sometimes we feel our ignorance is simply misinformation, or caused by apathy or too much motivation. As Carlyle Marney asked; "Do not all have Ph.D's in mis-knowing, notknowing and unknowing?"[4] All of us want to excuse ourselves by saying, "I just didn't know."

---

4   Carlyle Marney, *He Became Like Us* (New York: Abingdon Press, 1964), 21.

Some Knew What They Were Doing

No, Jesus was not offering a simple excuse. He was not praying: "Excuse them, God. They didn't really know." If we are going to be honest, the Roman soldiers knew exactly what they were doing. Crucifixion was their job. They didn't pay any attention to Jesus. To them, he was just another criminal. They may have thought he was a Jewish prophet, who had led a group of people in an insurrection against the Roman government. They drove the nails in his hands and feet and crucified him to put an end to his work. The Roman leaders knew what they were doing.

Pilate washed his hands of this Jesus problem. He didn't want to make a decision. He wanted to be on the sidelines. The high priests knew what they were doing. They wanted to get rid of Jesus because they thought he was a heretic. He was causing them constant trouble by challenging their teachings and traditions. Their answer was to stop him. These words do not imply that those who crucified him bear no responsibility for their actions.

Unaware of Who Jesus Was

What then do these words mean? "Father, forgive them, for they don't know what they are doing." Jesus was saying that these persons who were crucifying him did not know the enormity of this event. They really did not know what they were doing. Do you think any person would crucify the Son of God if he or she really knew who he was? Of course not! They did not really know who was hanging there. They didn't sense that this was truly God's Son.

Seldom Aware of the Responsibility of Our Actions

We have that same problem with our sins, too, don't we? Who would ever take the first drink, if he or she knew that this drink might lead him or her to become an alcoholic? Who would ever stick a drug needle in their arm or take some dope, if they thought they would become addicted? Who would ever engage in an illicit sex act, if he or she thought they would go down a path of promiscuity? But much of our life is charted by those kinds of decisions.

When we begin to pull on the thread in the garment of life, before we know it, the whole garment has begun to unravel. We fail to realize that all sin is an affront to God. All of our sin ultimately is a sin against God. King David said about his sin, "Lord, I have sinned against thee and against thee only have I sinned" (II Samuel 12:13). Whatever our sin is, it is a sin against God. Our sins affect us personally, as well as others, but most of all they affect God. Your sins and mine were part of the sin that Jesus had to bear on his cross.

RECEIVING FORGIVENESS

The Costly Nature of Forgiveness

Then fourthly, how do you and I receive the grace about which Jesus speaks in God's forgiveness? It begins, I think, in an awareness of the costly nature of forgiveness. Forgiveness is an easy matter for many, until they have someone to forgive; then they begin to see how difficult it is.

Do you remember several years ago when the Pope was wounded by a man who tried to assassinate him? The Pope forgave the man who attempted to assassinate him. It was interesting to read some of the letters to the editor in *Time Magazine*. One of them wrote: "It is the Pope's business to forgive." That is the way many feel about God. It is just his business to forgive.

C. S. Lewis wrote a number of years ago about the terrible duty of forgiveness.

> Everyone says forgiveness is a lovely idea until they have something to forgive, as we had during the war. And then to mention the subject at all is to be greeted with howls of anger. It is not that people think this too high and difficult a virtue. It is that they think it hateful and contemptible. 'That sort of talk makes them sick,' they say. And half of you want to ask

me, 'I wonder how you'd feel about forgiving the Gestapo if you were a Pole or a Jew?'[5]

Forgiveness is so easy until we have to forgive someone. Then it becomes very difficult. When someone has hurt you, or they have sinned against you, or you against another, it then often becomes very difficult to forgive.

When I was a pastor in a university community a number of years ago, I received a telephone call informing me about a college student who was in the hospital. Our church was only about two blocks away from the university, and many students attended our church. I was asked if I would go to the hospital and see her. She had attempted suicide. As I talked with this young woman, I discovered that she had attempted suicide because she was pregnant. She was only a sophomore in college, still single, of course, and didn't know what to do. She had been so frightened, and didn't think she could tell anyone about her situation. We talked for a long time, and I asked her if she wanted me to call her parents. "Yes," she finally said. It was the only thing she knew to do. "They will never understand," she said. "They will never forgive me."

I got on the telephone and called a pastor friend of mine in the city where her parents lived. I knew they were members of his church. I asked him how they would react. "I don't know," he said. "I just played golf today with her father. Her father has a violent temper." I asked him to have her parents come to see me first and let me talk with them. They did. I explained to them the situation and told them that this was a time not to reject their daughter, but a time for them to reach out with compassion, love, and support. Their daughter needed their love, understanding, and forgiveness. I couldn't make them do that, but I hoped they would. After talking with the parents, I went with them to the hospital. We met with the young woman and talked. It was a difficult and emotional time. But the student's parents accepted her, and expressed their love to her. Later they left the hospital, went home and tried to rebuild

---

5   C. S. Lewis, *Mere Christianity* (New York: The Macmillan Co., 1943), 89, Book III.

their lives. But it wasn't easy for the young woman or her parents. Forgiveness was very costly. Forgiveness is never easy for any of us.

AN ACKNOWLEDGMENT OF SIN

Forgiveness begins with an acknowledgment of our sin. "All have sinned" (Romans 3:25), the Scriptures declare. Our confession is an acknowledgment that our sins have helped put Jesus Christ on the cross. We, too, share in the sins of humanity. The sins of humanity cost God the incarnation and the suffering death of his Son. The Word became flesh and identified with humanity. God's sacrifice to bring us forgiveness is beyond belief. It is indeed matchless grace. God's costly sacrifice should remind us of the horror of sin. There cannot be forgiveness without the recognition that sin is an awful act in God's sight.

I like the prayer of Eric Milner White, which he adapted from one of the prayers of John Donne.

> Forgive me, O Lord
> O Lord forgive me my sins,
> the sins of my youth,
> the sins of the present;
> the sins I laid upon myself in an ill pleasure,
> the sins I cast upon others in an ill example;
> the sins which are manifest to all the world,
> the sins which I have laboured
>   to hide from mine acquaintance,
>   from my own conscience,
>   and even from my memory;
>   my crying sins and my whispering sins,
>   my ignorant sins and my willful;
> sins against my superiors, equals, servants,
>   against my lovers and benefactors,
>   sins against myself, mine own body, my own soul;
> sins against thee,

O Almighty Father,
O merciful Son,
O blessed Spirit of God.[6]

ACCEPT GOD'S ACCEPTANCE OF US

To receive forgiveness, we begin with an acknowledgment that we are sinners. But we have to do more than acknowledge our sins. We have to accept God's forgiveness. We have to accept our acceptance by God. This acceptance is an affirmation that even in our sinfulness we are not abandoned by God. Our sins need not destroy us, but we can be set free from them and become new persons again through God's forgiveness.

If Jesus Christ could ask for forgiveness of others in his dying moments on the cross, look at the message that reveals to us about the forgiving grace of God. But you and I have to be willing to accept that forgiveness. We can't just think about it, talk about it, preach about it, hear about it, or sing about it. We must accept God's forgiveness if it is to be meaningful for us.

In 1830 a man named George Wilson killed a government agent while he was trying to rob the U. S. mail. He was sentenced to be hanged. President Andrew Jackson gave him a pardon. But George Wilson did a strange thing. He turned the pardon down. Nobody knew what to do then. What do you do with a man who has turned down a pardon? His case went all the way to the Supreme Court. At that time Chief Justice Marshall made this ruling: "A pardon is a slip of paper, the value of which is determined by the acceptance of the person to be pardoned. If it is refused, it is no pardon. George Wilson must be hanged." And he was!

The forgiveness of God must be accepted. You and I must open our hearts and lives to God and receive his grace, if it will benefit us.

---

6   Quoted in Richard Holloway, *The Killing: Meditations on the Death of Jesus* (Wilton, Connecticut.: Morehouse Barlow, 1984), 39-40.

HAVING BEEN FORGIVEN, WE FORGIVE OTHERS

Having received God's pardon, then we in turn have to forgive others. The only petition in the Lord's Prayer that has any condition to it is the one that says, "Forgive us our trespasses as we forgive those who have trespassed against us" (Mark 11:26). A closed heart or a closed mind the unwillingness to forgive others blocks our own relationship to God and closes the door to our own ability to receive God's forgiveness. The woman who said, "I'll forgive but I won't forget," hasn't really experienced forgiveness. Having experienced God's forgiveness, we cannot refuse to forgive others. To be unforgiving is to inhibit God's grace in our own lives. Our refusal closes the door to God's love toward us.

Several years ago when I had an opportunity to be in England, I visited the Coventry Cathedral. This cathedral was completely destroyed by German bombs in the Second World War. After the war, the cathedral was rebuilt. In the ruins of the old cathedral, which is preserved as an outdoor chapel, stands a wooden cross which was constructed from timbers out of the burned out cathedral. On these two charred pieces of wood there are two words: "Father forgive." They reflect the spirit of our Lord.

Jesus hanging on the cross cried: "Father forgive them for they know not what they do." Those words include you and me. Thank God they do.

CHAPTER 2

THE PROMISE THAT LIFE GOES ON

LUKE 23:32-43

On Boot Hill outside Old Virginia City, Montana, there are five graves in a row all marked the same way with name and date except one which has one word the others do not bear. Vigilantes had hanged these men because of their slaughter of lonely travelers from the mines outside the town. On one of these markers are these words:

> "Haze Lyons
> Hanged
> Jan. 14
> 1864
> Peccavi."

The word Peccavi is Latin for "I have sinned." But it didn't make any difference whether he confessed that he had sinned or not, he was still hanged.

WHO WERE THESE TWO THIEVES?

There were two thieves who also had sinned. They were put to death in the first century by Roman soldiers. Jesus Christ was nailed to a cross between these two thieves. Scholars have debated what kind of criminals these two men may have been. Some scholars have speculated that they were just common criminals thieves or robbers.

Others have argued that the persons the Romans usually crucified were those involved in revolts to overthrow the government
of Rome. These two men may have been Zealots, who wanted
to overthrow the military power of Rome. If so, they may have
organized guerilla warfare and worked behind the scenes where
they committed robbery for money to finance their attack against
the Roman government. These men of violence had resorted to
stealing to fulfill their goals. They had failed. Legend has called
the penitent thief Dismas and the thief who railed against Jesus
was named Gesmas. Three voices from those crosses are still being
heard centuries later. Let's listen to what these three voices said and
see if there is a message for us.

THE VOICE OF RIDICULE

The first voice was a retreat into ridicule. With a loud voice,
he joined the soldiers and the crowd as they mocked Jesus. "If. . .
if you really are the King of the Jews, as that inscription on your
cross says," he jeered, "then you climb down from your cross and
save yourself and us." "If you really are a big-shot king, now is the
time to show it."

GOD, DO SOMETHING!

That refrain, however, is not limited to the past. I have heard
these words and you have heard them. We have heard them from
others and sometimes they have been your words and mine. From
a hospital bed, a man dying with cancer looked up at me and said:
"Preacher, if your God can do anything, get him to heal me of this
cancer." A father looked up at me from his chair beside the bed
of his young daughter, who had an incurable cancer and said: "If
. . .if God loves us, why won't he make my daughter well?" H. G.
Wells goes even further in one of his novels when one of his char-
acters exclaims: "If there is a God who looks down on all the evil
and suffering in the world and could do something and doesn't, I
would spit into his empty face." Oh, yes, there are still voices that

join with this thief from the first century: "If you are God, then do something!"

JESUS COULD NOT SAVE HIMSELF

But Jesus could not save himself. He had spent several hours the night before in the Garden of Gethsemane wrestling with his sense of destiny. He prayed: "Now is my soul troubled; and what shall I say? 'Father, save me from this hour?' But for this cause came I to this hour" (John 12:27). The Scriptures have always declared that Jesus was not just a victim on that cross. In some unique way he has borne the sins of humanity. The cross was inevitable. "On him has been laid the iniquity of us all" (Isaiah 53:6). There was something else going on at this cross other than just a victim being nailed to a stake. In a unique way, God was identifying with the sufferings of humanity and bearing our suffering and pain. He could not save himself and save us, and he knew that well.

A PENITENT VOICE

Quickly, however, another voice, that of Dismas responded: "We deserved everything we have received. Why are you taunting Jesus this way? We chose our own path. We decided to be criminals, and we walked down that way. We wanted to be revolutionaries, and we got caught."

WE BEAR RESPONSIBILITY FOR OUR ACTIONS

It has always amazed me how many persons can never see his or her responsibility in determining what has happened to them. A woman asked me in the hospital one day: "What have I done that God has punished me this way? Why did God give me lung cancer?" At the very moment she was asking me that question, she was still smoking a cigarette as she had done for thirty years. She chose her path, but tried to place the responsibility for her illness on God.

Sometimes we blame God for what we ourselves have done to our body. Overeating, excessive smoking and drinking, and the lack of exercise may be the primary factor in our poor health and not "God's will." We have voiced the wrong question when we ask: "Why did God do this to me?" Let's not blame God when we have chosen our own pathway.

WHERE WERE OTHERS WHO COULD HELP JESUS?

Jesus could not save himself. But where were all the people Jesus had helped? Where were they? Why didn't they come rushing to his side? Where were Peter, James and John, and the other disciples? Why didn't they stand by his side? Where was Zacchaeus, who said that Jesus had done so much for him that he gave back half of all his money to the people he had cheated. Where was Lazarus? Where was the centurion whose daughter Jesus had healed when she lay near death? Where was the demoniac? Where was the blind man, the lame man, and the deaf man? Where were the hundreds of people whom Jesus had helped? Like a crystal bowl dropped on a brick walk, they were scattered and shattered. Their voices are mute—silenced in the shadows afraid, silenced by the jeers of the crowds, unwilling to step forward. They could not save him either.

A CRY OF HELP TO JESUS

The second voice we hear from the cross is a desperate cry for help. "Jesus, remember me when you come into your Kingdom." Jesus! He used the name Jesus! Nobody else in the gospels, other than the mother of Jesus used that name for him. And Mary used it when Jesus was a child. Our Lord was called either Jesus, Master, Jesus of Nazareth, Rabbi, Teacher, Jesus the son of David or Jesus the son of Joseph. Even his disciples did not call our Lord by that name.

The use of the familiar childhood name of Jesus raises an interesting question. Does it imply that this thief may have known Jesus when he was a boy? Were they childhood friends whose friendship went back many years? We don't know. But this familiar, personal reference may indicate some kind of past friendship.

THE KINGDOM OF GOD

"Remember me when you come into your kingdom." How did he know about Jesus' kingdom? Had he heard Jesus preach about the Kingdom of God? In dozens of parables he may have heard Jesus say the "Kingdom of Heaven is like. . ." Had he heard Jesus speak about his kingly reign, but he had decided that he wanted to see if he could usher in God's kingdom by violence? He may have thought he could overthrow the Roman government and establish God's reign with a strong arm.

Now, while he was hanging on a cross, he realized that his way of violence was not going to work. In his dying moments, he turned to the One whose message offered a different hope. "Jesus, remember me when you come into your kingdom." He now realized that Jesus' kingdom might be the way that God would rule his people.

WHY DOES HE RESPOND AT THE CROSS OF JESUS?

Why did this thief turn in this moment to Jesus? Why would he believe Jesus when he was hanging on a cross and dying like he was? Why would he believe in Jesus now when he had not believed in him before? I don't know. What has there been about Jesus Christ hanging on a cross that has always attracted men and women to him and brought them to God? Men and women down through the ages have seen something unique in the Christ figure hanging on a cross, suffering for humanity between heaven and earth. The same thing that happened to him has happened to countless others through the centuries. Before the thief died, he was the last to see Jesus on the cross and the first to experience the redemption of the Christ on the cross. The crucified Christ continues to draw men and women to God.

Remember Me

"Remember me." Listen to his plea: "Remember me." Those words fell like a pewter platter which had been dropped on a slate floor and have echoed down through the centuries. "Remember me." These words are your cry and mine. When we come to moments of loneliness and rejection, and nobody seems to understand us or care, we cry: "Remember me, Lord." When we come to the times in our life when we have lost our job or are frustrated in our work, we cry: "Remember me." When we have experienced an illness or heard those dreaded words from our doctor, "It is cancer," we cry: "Remember me." When we feel misunderstood or rejected by friends or relatives, we cry: "Remember me." When we stand by the grave of a loved one or a friend, or know that we have come to our own time of dying, we join the words of the penitent thief and say: "Jesus, remember me."

A Personal Plea

The thief without hesitation pled, "Remember me." His plea was very personal. His request was not just for a nation, or for a group of people, or Israel, but it was: "Remember me." There are times it is o.k. to voice very personal pleadings with God. Martin Luther, the great reformer, said that the personal pronouns are the heart of our faith. The twentythird Psalm rings with them. "The Lord is *my* shepherd. *I* shall not want. He makes *me* to lie down. He restores *my* soul." There comes in every life a sense of "myness" in which we want to be remembered by God. As he faced the certainty of his own death, the thief knew it was time to face his own personal need unashamedly.

In the small book, *Dear God: Children's Letters to God*, an eleven year old boy writes, "Dear God, I was watching T.V. when the Challenger shuttle exploded. That was a sad time. Was there anything you could have done? Were you mad because they came too close to your territory? We're sorry, Jose."[1]

Oh, Jose, God doesn't cause those accidents. God was present with those people in their moment of death. He is with you and me and will be with us when we face our own death. We worship a God who is concerned about you, me, and everyone. "Remember me," he prayed.

A Voice of Forgiveness

The third voice from the cross—the voice of Jesus was an answer to prayer. Earlier we noted that the first words from the cross were the prayer of Jesus. These second words were a response to the prayer from the penitent thief. Was it too late for him to pray? There he was hanging on a cross a few hours before he was to die. The thief made what we might call a deathbed confession. Was the thief's plea too late? The response from Jesus indicates that it was not too late.

The penitent thief is the patron saint for all those who have come to the end of their rope and feel there is no hope. When all seemed lost, Jesus reached out to him and extended his love and grace. This was a clear affirmation that salvation is by grace. As long as a man or woman has a mind to think and breath to breathe, he or she has opportunity to respond to God. No matter how hopeless, dejected or depraved regardless of how far down the road one is, God is still there extending his love and grace.

Jesus: A Friend to Sinners

This penitent thief symbolized that Jesus is a friend of all sinners. Earl Ellis writes in his commentary that this incident in Luke's gospel is the core of this episode about the crucifixion. "The bandit is representative of the type of person Jesus has come to

---

1   David Heller, *Dear God: Children's Letters to God* (New York: Bantam Books, 1987), 38.

save."[2] This thief symbolizes all the sinners Christ has come to save. Throughout Luke's gospel, the message is that Jesus reaches out to all sinners. Jesus said, "I have come to seek and save that which is lost" (Luke 19:10). "Those who are healthy don't need a physician" (Luke 5:31), Jesus said. Jesus reached out to persons in every walk of life to bring them grace, hope, love, and forgiveness. This thief is representative of all sinners. His plight indicates that no person can be too far away from God that he/she is not acceptable.

JESUS' WORDS OF ASSURANCE

A Definite Time

Listen to what he told this penitent thief. He first gave him immediate assurance. *"Today* you will be with me in Paradise." Today! Why he had only asked to be remembered something indefinite yet Jesus gave him a concrete time. "Today." Jesus gave him far more than he asked for. But isn't that what God always does for us. There is a sense of immediacy in Jesus' reply.

A Personal Plea

Notice further Jesus' response. "This day *you* will be with me." "You." Here is a personal pledge from Jesus. He told the thief, "You are important." This is a positive word for all of us. "Remember," Jesus said to the penitent thief, "You are important to God. You will experience this togetherness with me in my kingdom. You will not be forgotten. You will *be*." The thief's personal plea was answered with a personal pledge.

---

2   E. Earle Ellis, *The Gospel of Luke, New Century Bible* (Greenwood, South Carolina: The Attic Press, Inc., 1974), 267.

THE IMPORTANCE OF PERSONS

Throughout the ministry of Jesus, he stressed the importance of persons. In various parables he affirmed the significance of persons. He noted how a shepherd would leave a hundred sheep and go search for the one lost sheep. In his parables about the lost coin and the lost son, Jesus affirmed the importance of a person's worth. Jesus reached out to the poor, rich, sick, well, lame, blind, deaf, weak, strong, men and women, young and old. Jesus asked the searching question: "What shall it profit a man (woman) if he (she) gains the whole world and loses his (her) own soul?" "Jesus alone in history," Emerson wrote, "estimated the greatness of man (woman)."

John Baillie is one of my favorite theologians. This Scottish theologian was principal for many years of New College and Dean of the Faculty of Divinity at Edinburgh University. In his book entitled, *And the Life Everlasting,* Baillie affirmed that the Christian does have hope not only in this life but in the life to come. He argued against the hopelessness and disenchantment which many feel in our modern society. He believed strongly that the Christian person would continue to exist beyond death. He based his argument on the fact that you and I have opportunity to enter in fellowship with God here. Because we can know God now and have fellowship with God, this means that we can be assured that we will know God later beyond death.

Baillie offers what he calls "a logic of hope." It reads like this: "If the individual can commune with God, then he must matter to God. If he matters to God, he must share God's eternity."[3] If you and I can relate to God in this life and commune with God through prayer, then we are important to God. If we are important to God in this life, God is not going to discard us when death comes. To Baillie, this is the only unanswerable argument for immortality.

---

3   John Baillie, *And the Life Everlasting* (New York: Charles Scribner's Sons, 1933), 163.

Jesus has assured us that this is true. "*You,*" Jesus said to the thief, "will be with me in Paradise."

PERSONAL COMPANIONSHIP

Notice the next step which is suggested by Jesus' response to the thief. In quiet confidence Jesus promised him that he would share his personal companionship. "You will be *with me.*" Isn't this the greatest promise of all? These words of Christ to the thief are directed to all of us. "Lo, I am with you always unto the end of the age" (Matthew 28:20). Jesus said to his disciples. "I am the resurrection and the life" (John 11:24). When you and I entrust our lives to Christ, we experience eternal life now. "This is eternal life," John wrote, "to know the Son" (John 17:3). To know the Son in this life opens the door to eternal life. Eternal life is not something that is given to us after death. It is a present possession. Death simply opens the door that enables us to experience eternity with God. Our communion with God begins here in this life. Our faith journey carries us out of this earthly life into eternity.

William Cosby Bell was professor for many years in the Virginia Theological Seminary in Richmond, Virginia. When Dr. Bell discovered that he was dying of a sudden illness, he sent a message to his former students at the seminary. He always referred to the young men as "boys."

> Tell the boys that I've grown surer of God every year of my life, and I've never been so sure as I am right now. I am so glad to find that I haven't the least shadow of shrinking or uncertainty. I have always thought so and now that I am right up against it, I know. Life owes me nothing. I've had work that I loved, and I've lived in a beautiful place among congenial friends. I've had love in its highest form and I've got it forever. I can see now that death is just the smallest thing, just an accident, but it means nothing. There is no real break, and life, all that really counts in life, goes on.

Dr. Bell had lived his life in faith and trust in the presence of Christ and when the trumpet sounded from the other side, his trust was still firm.

LIFE GOES ON

Jesus said, "You will be with me in Paradise." Here is the assurance that life for the Christian does go on. Death is not the end, but it is a door that opens into eternity where we can be with God. Death is not an exit but an entrance. The word "paradise" is an old Persian word that is used only two other places in the New Testament. II Corinthians 12:3 reads: "And I know that this man was caught up into Paradise whether in the body or out of the body I do not know, God knows." The other is found in the Book of Revelation 2:7: "To him who conquers I will grant to eat of the tree of life, which is in the paradise of God."

Paradise is a word that depicts a walled garden or an enclosed park. This word is similar to the reference to "Abraham's bosom," which is used in Luke 16:22. This word refers to the Garden of Eden—a place of blessedness—a place where God is. Paradise affirms one's sense of being in the presence of God. Jesus was promising the thief that when he died he would be ushered into the presence of God the Father, and it would be a wonderful experience.

"I am going to prepare a place for you," Jesus told his disciples. You and I can rest in the assurance of God's love and grace. With the Lord as our shepherd, we can believe that we shall not want and we shall dwell in the house of the Lord forever.

There are some who teach that life comes to a dead end. We simply become extinct. There are others who say that we will be reincarnated as some lower form of life like an insect or an animal. Still others teach that we are simply absorbed into God and with this merger we lose our own identity. The Christian faith affirms that when we die in Jesus Christ there is eternal life. The Christian who began his or her life with Christ in this world will continue that life with him in eternity. Eternal life is not something that is conferred at death, but it is a present possession.

Our Salvation Is In a Particular Cross

Look at the three crosses on the hill of ancient Calvary. Remember that our salvation is not found in crosses alone. Thousands of crosses have been planted on Roman hillsides. Sometimes these crosses were placed so closely together that people could hardly walk past them. They would often be stretched for miles along a roadside when a nation tried to revolt against Rome. Our redemption is not in crosses alone. Our salvation is brought about by one particular person who died on a cross—Jesus Christ.

As you look to this Jesus who died on his cross, remember that sometimes one person may respond to him, like the penitent thief, and another reject him, like the other thief did. Why didn't he repent? He witnessed the death of Christ. He heard his words just like the other thief did. For some reason, his heart was hardened and his lips could not voice a prayer. He was so near but still unmoved, so close but so far away. He was untouched like others still are today. But all of us, you and I alike, are searching, like the penitent thief, to be remembered and to find some kingdom in life. We, too, wonder where life is going and what the purpose of it all is. Let us seek to find the answers in God's love and grace. Remember that life does go on when we die in Christ. We can simply die, or we can die in Christ. N. T. Wright has reminded us that "meditation on Jesus' suffering and death becomes a vital and central way of celebrating and gaining access to the free, forgiving, healing love of the creator God."[4]

Quiet Confidence

On the tomb of the astronomer, Copernicus, in Freudenberg, Prussia, carved in Latin, are the following words freely translated:

---

4   Marcus J. Borg and N. T. Wright, *The Meaning of Jesus: Two Visions* (San Francisco: Harper Collins Paperback, 2000), 106.

"I ask not such favor as St. Paul received nor yet such grace as St. Peter obtained; But what, on the cross, to the thief You did give, O Jesus, I fervently pray, grant to me."

We can all make that our prayer as we face our own death. With quiet confidence, we can ask to be remembered by the God who loved us and sent his Son to die for us.

John Todd was a nineteenth century Congregational minister who served in New England. He was reared by his aunt who took him into her home when he was left an orphan when he was six years old. She helped him get his education at Yale University and Yale Divinity School. Later he went on to be pastor in Pittsfield, Massachusetts. While he was in Pittsfield, he received a rather pitiful letter from his aunt. She told him that she had incurable cancer and knew that death was imminent for her. She reminded him that he was a college and seminary graduate and a minister, had read many books, and was a wise person. Could he tell her something about death and if she had anything to fear?

In the letter Todd wrote to his aunt, he responded: "It is now thirtyfive years since I, a little boy of six, was left quite alone in the world. You sent me word that you would give me a home and be a kind mother to me. I have never forgotten the day when I made the long journey of ten miles from my home in Killingsworth to your home in North Killingsworth. I can still recall my disappointment when I learned that instead of coming for me yourself you had sent your colored man Caesar to fetch me. I can still remember my tears and anxiety as, perched on your horse and clinging tight to Caesar, I started for your house."

Then Todd went on to write about his childish fear of the darkness, and whether his aunt would still be up waiting for him since it was so late. He remembered coming out of the woods into a clearing and seeing a friendly candle glowing in the window and his aunt waiting at the door. He recalled her warm arms around him and gently lifting a tired and bewildered little boy down from the horse. She gave him a good meal beside the warm bright fire and took him to his room and sat beside him until he went to sleep.

His letter continued: "You are probably wondering why I am now recalling all these things to your mind. Some day soon God will send for you, to take you to a new home. Don't fear the summons, the strange journey, the messenger of death. At the end of the road you will find a love and a welcome; you will be safe in God's care and keeping. God can be trusted trusted to be as kind to you as you were to me so many years ago."[5]

Let us walk out on that footbridge of faith over the chasm of uncertainty and death with the assurance that God will sustain us. Trust God. I know that God will not let us down.

5   James Gordon Gilkey, "Christianity's Message to the Modern World," *The American Pulpit Series 6* (New York: AbingdonCokesbury Press, 1945), 50-53.

CHAPTER 3

Words of Human Devotion

John 19:25-27

The first three words of Jesus from the cross, as he was dying, were all directed to others. The first word was a prayer offered for his enemies. "Father, forgive them for they know not what they do." The second word gave hope to the penitent thief. "This day you will be with me in Paradise." And the third word demonstrated concern for his mother, as Jesus asked John to care for his mother.

The Women at The Cross

Note the women who were at the cross. There is some confusion among scholars as to exactly how many women were really at the foot of the cross. It is not clear whether John was referring to three or four women. If there were three, the list would read: Mary (Jesus' mother), Mary's sister Mary of Clopas, and Mary Magdalene. It seems unlikely to me, however, that there would be two sisters in the same family named Mary. So more likely there were four women. Among these were Mary, the mother of Jesus, Mary of Clopas, the mother of James and Joseph, Mary Magdalene, and the sister of Mary, who was not named. I think this woman was the mother of the writer of the Gospel of John. John remained in the background in his gospel. He never referred to himself other than as the beloved disciple. He did not speak of this woman as "my" mother, but just Mary's sister. These were the four women who were gathered near the cross of Jesus.

John also presents us a bit of a problem here when he wrote that these women were "near" the cross. Matthew, Mark, and Luke all state that the women were some distance "away" from the cross. What do we have here? Is this another one of those irreconcilable problems in the Bible? I really don't think so. Both emphases could be true at different times in the story of the crucifixion.

The synoptic writers may have written about the early stages of the crucifixion when the women probably hung back to avoid the horrors of seeing Jesus being stretched out on his cross. They probably had no desire to witness the nails being driven into the hands and feet of Jesus or watch his cross lifted up and dropped into its hole in the ground. But once the cross was set in place, the women moved closer to it. Some New Testament scholars have found evidence which has indicated that relatives and friends could gather near the cross during the final hours before the crucified person died.[1]

It is interesting that women were present at the cross. Only women were there, except for John, who was likely a very young man at this time. None of the other male disciples were anywhere to be found. They had all fled. Oh, some have tried to pass this fact off glibly and assert that the women were there because there was no personal threat to them. I do not think that is true. Any time a person, male or female, chose to associate himself or herself with a revolutionary person, that person was in danger. Jesus was being crucified because he had been accused of being a revolutionary figure who wanted to overthrow the Roman government.

Later these same women likely helped in the burial of Jesus. Some of these women were also among the first persons who took the initiative on Easter Sunday morning to go to the grave and bring more spices to anoint Jesus' body. Having taken the initiative to go to Jesus' tomb, they were the first ones to see the risen Lord. Jesus, on the other hand, took the initiative to disclose himself to the male disciples.

---

1   Eduard Stauffer, *Jesus and His Story* (London: SCM Press, 1960), 111 and 179.

Women Were Among the Followers of Jesus

Considering what a male dominated world it was in the day of Jesus, there is, nevertheless, clear evidence that there were women among the disciples of Jesus. Mary and Martha clearly were disciples, learners of Jesus' teaching. Mary Magdalene was another. They were not among the twelve, but they were a part of the wider circle of believers. Paul's ministry in various churches included women like Lydia, Phoebe, the deacon mentioned in the Roman Epistle, and Priscilla, the wife of Aquila referred to in I Corinthians. There are others mentioned like Euodia and Syntyche in Philippians. These women and others were all servants in the ministry of Christ.

Women have always made a difference in the church. In my many years in ministry, I have often found women among the most faithful disciples that Jesus has in the church today. Women are some of the finest religious thinkers in the church. They are among the most open, most teachable, and most committed to God. And I believe that this has been true since the first century. What would the church be without the women who labor continuously in its ministry?

The Task of the Roman Soldiers

Contrast the four women with the four soldiers at the cross of Jesus. The soldiers had a ghastly, bloody task. Who would want it? They had to stretch men out on a wooden cross and nail spikes through their hands and feet. All the time the soldiers were doing their job, the men they were crucifying were cursing and screaming at them. The family members, who were sometimes standing nearby at the cross, tried to stop them and hurled taunts and jeers at them. They were spat upon and the recipient of every vile abuse you can possibly imagine. What soldier would want that duty?

DIVIDING JESUS' CLOTHING

Because the assignment was so despicable, the soldiers were given the spoils of the persons they put to death. As a token reward for their nasty work, they got to keep the clothing of the person they crucified. A male in the day of Jesus usually had five pieces of clothing: A headpiece, a robe, a tunic underneath the robe, a belt or girdle, and sandals. The soldiers divided the garments among themselves.

When the soldiers came to the tunic—the undergarment— however, they found that it had been woven without seams. They felt it would ruin the garment to divide it. They decided to gamble to see who could get the seamless tunic. Jesus' tunic was most likely made by his mother. Can you imagine her reaction as she saw the soldiers casting dice to see who would get the garment that she had made for her Son. John saw this as a fulfillment of Scripture and quoted Psalm 22:18.

THE SYMBOLISM OF JESUS' ROBE

Scholars have seen all kinds of symbolism in this seamless garment of Jesus. Some have said that it stood for the seamless robe of the high priest. It was a sign that Jesus was not only a king but the high priest. Others have seen this seamless garment as a sign of the unity of the church. You have heard some of the fanciful stories about the robe of Jesus. Lord Douglas wrote a novel, entitled *The Robe,* in which he spun a long tale about Jesus' robe and all the magical things that happened to persons who came in contact with it. Whittier expressed that view in these lines:

> The healing of His seamless dress
> Is by our beds of pain;
>   We touch Him in life's throng and press;
>   And we are whole again.[2]

2   John Greenleaf Whittier, "Our Master," in *Masterpieces of Religious Verse* (New York: Harper & Brothers Publishers, 1948), 237.

THE SUFFERING SERVANT

Remember the woman who reached out and touched the hem of Jesus' robe so she could be healed. But the power was not in the robe. The problem with this symbolism is that we have to note that it was not his robe that was seamless in the first place. It was his tunic, his undergarment. Secondly, the soldiers had taken his tunic away from him. He had not given it up. All of this symbolism borders on nonsense. What is really happening here is that a man is stripped naked and left hanging on a cross to die.

The real picture is of the Suffering Servant at his highest. Here is the picture of One who had been stripped of all of his garments and sacrificed his life for humanity. Here is the towel and the basin symbol of the servant role at its highest. This is the supreme example of suffering for others. There was no power in his garments. The power was in the Christ, and he died on his cross as he hung between heaven and earth.

WOMAN, BEHOLD YOUR SON

Hanging on that cross, Jesus looked down and saw his mother standing by and said: "Woman, behold your son." Jesus likely then nodded toward John. Many of us are taken aback by Jesus' phrase, "woman." Why didn't Jesus say, "Mother?" The use of "woman" sounds harsh and abrupt to us. But the word "woman" in Greek is a word of respect. It is the same word that Jesus used for his mother at the wedding at Cana. It was the same word Homer, the poet, put on the lips of Odysseus as he expressed affectionately his deep love for his wife, Penelope. "Lady" might be a good translation. "Dear lady, behold your son." Jesus was being respectful of his mother and was not being rude or abrupt.

WHERE WERE THE BROTHERS AND SISTERS OF JESUS?

But where were Jesus' brothers and sisters at this time? Why must John, not a member of his own family, become son? According to the Scriptures, Jesus had at least five brothers and two sisters. Where were they? None were at the cross. Some have tried to say that this was clear evidence that they were all stepbrothers and stepsisters of Jesus, children of an earlier marriage by Joseph. I think not. The gospel writers could easily have used the Greek word for stepbrothers and stepsisters. There is a word in Greek for stepchildren. But they did not use it.

WHY WAS JOHN SELECTED?

Why did Jesus select John? I think John was chosen because of the division which sometimes occurs in families by the loyalty which Christ claims upon a person's life. Mary continued to stand by her Son even at the cross. But the rest of Jesus' family at this point was not committed to Christ. They couldn't understand him or his message about God's kingdom. Mary had lived with this divisiveness for a long time. There had been a long history of misunderstanding Jesus. This problem had started early with Jesus.

The first record of this struggle occurred when Mary and Joseph had to go back a day's journey to the temple in Jerusalem where Jesus, a lad of twelve, was found discussing religion with the rabbis. When his parents asked him why he had caused them this problem, he told them: "I must be in my Father's house" (Luke 2:49). Later at a wedding feast in Cana, Mary asked Jesus to do something to keep the family from being embarrassed because of the shortage of wine. Jesus said: "Woman, what is this to you? My hour has not yet come" (John 2:112). When Jesus returned to his hometown of Nazareth, Mary's heart must have been filled with pride and hope. But her hopes were soon dashed to the ground by the angry, violent reaction of the townspeople as they attempted to cast Jesus off a precipice outside the village and kill him.

What Was Mary Thinking?

Rumors soon began to spread throughout the countryside about Jesus. Some people thought he was insane. At one point in his ministry, Mary and his brothers went to Jesus to try and bring him back home. But Jesus would not even come to the door and speak to them. His family did not know what to make of his behavior (Mark 3:31-35). Only a few months later Mary now stands at the foot of the cross where Jesus is dying. Mary, like all mothers, expected her son to outlive her. Now his dream of ushering in God's kingdom seemed to be collapsing with his crucifixion. Did she recall the words from Simeon when she had taken the baby Jesus to the temple to be dedicated and he told her that one day a sword would pierce her heart (Luke 2:35)? But in spite of it all, she was still there standing by the cross of Jesus. What was she thinking as she saw Jesus hanging on a cross?

Holman Hunt has a moving painting called "The Shadow of Death." It depicts a scene where Jesus is a young adult who is working as a carpenter in his shop during "the silent years." The young carpenter is stretching himself to relax his muscles at his workbench. The sun is shining through the doorway across his body and cast a shadow of the cross on the wall behind him. Mary, his mother, stands nearby, and her face is filled with horror and fear as she looks upon that shadow.

Do you think Mary really had anticipated Jesus' horrible death? I don't think so. None of the disciples had. They really didn't understand Jesus' prophecy about going up to Jerusalem to suffer and die. None of them had really anticipated this happening.

Behold, Your Mother

Jesus turned his head and looked at John the beloved disciple and said: "Behold, your mother." Scholars have had a field day with these statements of Jesus to Mary and John. Roman Catholic theologians, even distinguished scholars like Raymond Brown, have surmised that what Jesus was doing at this moment was making

Mary not only the "mother" of John but the mother of all the disciples, and hence the spiritual mother of the church. She is the Lady Zion.[3] All Christians then would be under her care as the mother of the church.

Other scholars have speculated that John, the beloved disciple, represents Gentile Christianity and Mary symbolizes Judaism, the ancient faith. She represents the heritage of Israel which is entrusted to and transformed by Christianity.[4] Everything of value and permanent significance in Judaism has now passed over into Christianity. This is symbolized in the fact that Mary now lives in the house of John.

JESUS' CONCERN FOR HIS MOTHER'S WELFARE

I think both of these views read too much into these words. I believe what is really happening here is Jesus' concern for his mother and her welfare after he dies. Before he died, Jesus simply wanted to arrange for his mother's future needs. Some scholars like Stauffer are convinced that the words Jesus used on the cross here are an official formulalike language of the Jewish law that provides for the protection of his mother.[5] A similar expression is found in the Tobit 7:12: "From now on you are her brother, behold she is your sister."[6] The words from Jesus may have been a kind of deathbed "will" to provide for his mother's protection. Jesus was saying in essence to John and Mary, "You be a son to Mary, John, and Mary will be a mother to you." These words reflect primarily love and concern.

---

3   Raymond E. Brown, *The Gospel According to John, XII-XXI* (Garden City, New York: Doubleday & Co., 1970), 923-927.
4   R. H. Strachan, *The Fourth Gospel* (London: SCM Press, 1951), 319.
5   Stauffer, *Jesus and His Story*, 113.
6   George R. BeasleyMurray, *John, Word Biblical Commentary* (Waco, Texas: Word Books, 1987), 349.

A COMMUNITY OF LOVE AND TRUST

But maybe there is still another insight discernible here. Can these words possibly be an insight into the nature of the beginning of the Church? The truth is that the Church was not founded on blood relationships but on love and trust. Anybody who really belongs to the family of the Church of Jesus Christ is a part of that community out of love, grace, and trust and not because he or she is somebody's relative. Jesus was establishing a new family. Remember Jesus' response on the occasion when his own family wanted to take him back home to Nazareth. He was told they were outside the house where he was but could not get to him because of the crowd. "Your mother and your brother are standing outside, desiring to see you." But he said to them, "My mother and my brothers are those who hear the word of God and do it" (Luke 8:20-21).

Jesus, you noticed, did not ask: "John, will you do this for me?" He just said, "Do it." He entrusted his mother to him. This is always the way Jesus comes to us, isn't it? He simply asks us to do something for him with the understanding and assurance that we will respond.

THE MINISTRY OF WOMEN TODAY

Where are the mothers and brothers of Jesus today? Oh, I can remember many of them in my life. And I'm sure you can as well. As I think back on the years I was a youth in my home church, most of the Sunday School teachers, mission workers, the choir directors (as we called them then), youth leaders, and other adult workers were mostly women. In every church where I have served as pastor I can point to women who have been among the real leaders, who touched my life in a positive way and made a difference in the ministry of that local church. I could name them for you, but those names would mean nothing to you. But all of these women have enriched my life spiritually. Now it is up to you and me. We are the mothers, sisters, brothers and sons in whom the ministry of the church has been entrusted. We are called to serve Jesus and minister in his name.

ANOTHER GLIMPSE OF MARY

John, most likely, soon took Mary away from that awful scene of her Son's death. The words of the spiritual have expressed it well: "Take my mother away. She doesn't need to watch this sorrow any longer." The only other time we read about Mary in the New Testament is in the first chapter of Acts. She was gathered with the rest of the disciples in the Upper Room where they were praying before Pentecost (Acts 1:1314). She was waiting with the other disciples for the coming of the Spirit of God after Jesus had ascended into Heaven. She was a part of the first Christian Church.

Tradition says that John lived for a while in Jerusalem and Mary stayed with him. She may have died soon afterwards or he may have even taken her with him to the Isle of Patmos. We do not know. There are no further records. Mary would have been a relatively young woman at the time of Jesus' death. She may have given birth to Jesus when she was twelve or thirteen. She was likely less than fifty years old when Jesus was crucified. This would make her still in the prime of life.

THE IMPORTANCE OF WOMEN IN THE MINISTRY OF JESUS

What can we now draw from all this discussion about Jesus' comments to his mother and John? I would suggest first that we recognize in this account the importance of women in the ministry of Jesus. They were central then, and still are today.

A small boy, probably not four years old, whose head could not reach the top of the counter, and whose chubby face still bore the remains of tears, asked in a quavering voice to the man behind the desk in the big department store: "Mister, have any mothers been turned in this morning?" The church needs to have a lot of mothers turned in today. We need mothers of all types and ages who will serve in the name of Christ in a wide variety of ministries, and fathers as well.

An Obligation to Care for Our Parents

Secondly, we note the concern that Jesus had for his mother's future care. Jesus took the fifth commandment seriously that we are "to honor our mothers and our fathers." No matter who we are, who our parents are, we have a responsibility, no, an obligation to care for our own parents.

The Significance of Temporal Needs

Thirdly, we, like our Lord, need to be concerned about temporal needs. Our physical wants and needs are important to God. What is all this nonsense about trying to separate our spiritual life from our temporal? The physical wellbeing of a widow, the elderly, the poor, the hungry, the needy are all important to God.

A Respect for Mary

Fourthly, this account conveys a deep respect for Mary. Oh, I don't think we should reverence or worship Mary. I not only have a profound sense of admiration for Mary as the mother of Jesus but a great feeling of gratitude. It is easy for us to stand two thousand years later and admire Mary. But too often we forget the insults, disrespect, and ridicule she likely had to bear when she told others that she was pregnant before she got married and tried to explain her predicament to others with stories about seeing angels. "Uh huh! Sure!" they would say! She likely had a very difficult time and probably had to endure a long period of disgrace. But in spite of all this, she established a home for Jesus where he experienced love, nurture and direction.

THE IMPORTANCE OF A MOTHER'S INFLUENCE

Mary's husband, Joseph, had likely been dead for some time. He was not mentioned as being alive during the ministry of Jesus. Mary seemed to be the major influence later in Jesus' life. One of the most important factors in the stability of a home is the love and guidance of a mother for her children. Charles and John Wesley, the founders of the Methodist church, were the devoted men they were, I believe, because of the mother they had and the powerful influence she had on their lives. A lot of fathers are often absent from the home. Our jobs consume us. Usually the mothers do most of the child rearing.

A number of years ago one of the universities in our country gave an honorary doctor's degree to a Niebuhr. Reinhold Niebuhr is considered by many scholars to have been one of the greatest theologians of the 20th century. He has continued to influence ethical thinking today. His brother, Richard Niebuhr and their sister Hulda were also recognized as outstanding theologians. But the honorary degree was not given to any of the children. This honorary degree was given to their mother. The aged mother, who had such a powerful influence upon these three children, was honored on this special occasion. She had produced in the same family, three of the most significant American theologians in the 20th century.

Don't sell yourself short, Mother! You can't begin to realize the impact you can have on your own children and others. Mary stood by Jesus, even when he was nailed to a cross. She loved him still.

THE COMMUNITY OF FAITH AND LOVE

Fifthly, we need to remember that the church is composed of those who belong to the family of God not out of inheritance or blood relationship but out of love and trust. The devotion of John and Mary for each other was a sign of the love which Christians could have for one another in the family of Christ's Church. God has demonstrated his love supremely in Jesus, and he has invited us to share in that continuing community of faith.

REPRESENTATIVES FOR OUR LORD

Finally, just as John was asked to represent Jesus for his mother, so now you and I are the representatives for our Lord in the world. John represented Jesus in his perpetual care of Mary as he made her a part of his own family. But now you and I, as a part of the family of Christ, are his representatives wherever we go in the world. Others will see what Christ is like through you and through me. John was present in the first century. You and I are here today. We are to live out our lives representing Christ.

Four preachers were discussing one day what they thought were the best translations of the Bible. One said that he liked the King James Version best because of the beauty of its language. Another said that he liked the Williams translation, because it was so exact in its translation of the Greek. Another said that he used the Good News Bible, because it put the biblical language in the every day language of the people. The fourth minister was silent for a while. Finally one of his fellow ministers asked: "What is your favorite translation?" "My favorite translation," he responded, "is my mother's." "Your mother has translated the Bible?" they asked. "Yes," he said. "She translated it into life every day in the way she lived, and it was the most convincing translation I ever read."

You and I translate Christ for others every day. I pray that what others read in your life and mine will be a good translation.

CHAPTER 4

THE CRY OF DERELICTION

MATTHEW 27:46-48

The woman sat in my study and began to weep uncontrolla-
bly." My husband, of some twenty years," she sobbed, "wrote me
a note last week saying that he had left me and the children for
another woman." She felt abandoned. The scene changes. A young
boy sat on a pile of rubble in El Salvador. A soldier went over to him
and asked him where his parents were. "They have been killed," the
boy responded. "Your brothers and sisters?" "They too are dead."
He was abandoned.

The scene changes again. A middleage woman had just hung
up the telephone from talking with her husband. They had planned
to have lunch together in a few minutes. But before she left her
office the telephone rang again. It was a neighbor calling. "Come
home quickly," she said. "Your husband has just had a heart attack!"
She rushed home. But when she got there, it was too late. He was
already dead. They had no children. She too felt abandoned.

CUT OFF FROM OUR ROOTS

Unfortunately, we all are too familiar with the feeling of being
abandoned. To feel forsaken is to experience being cut off from
one's roots—a sense of being alone. There is often a feeling of
emptiness, depression, and absence of meaning. "What's the point
of going on?" the perplexed person cries. Some of you may have
experienced a feeling of being "forsaken" when you moved into
a new community and knew no one, or went away to college, or

overseas in the military service. You may have had those feelings at work or at school. An adolescent struggles with a sinking feeling as he or she tries to grow up thinking, "No one understands me or cares about me."

A friend told me recently that life had become very difficult at work for him. He had made some hard decisions, and now when he walked down the hallway, his colleagues would no longer speak to him. A wall of silence had been erected between them. He was ignored. He understood the feeling of being abandoned.

THE AGONIZING QUESTIONS: WHY?

We, too, with Jesus ask: "My God, why?" Why do these things happen? Why is there pain, suffering, agony, and conflict in the world? There are no easy answers. These agonizing questions have echoed down through the centuries, "Why?"

In Archibald MacLeish's Pulitzer prize winning play, *J.B.,* which is based on the Book of Job, Sarah, the wife of J. B., struggled to understand why their children had died and why they had suffered so much. Out of her pain Sarah cries:

> "Go! Go where?
> If there were darkness I'd go there.
> If there were night I'd lay me down in it.
> God has shut the night against me.
> God has set the dark alight
> With horror blazing blind as day
> When I go toward it. . .
> Close my eyes.

Then J. B. responds:
> "If I Knew. . . If I knew why! . . .
> What I can't bear is the blindness
> Meaninglessness the numb blow
> Fallen in the stumbling night.[1]

1   Archibald MacLeish, *J. B.* (Boston: Houghton Mifflin Co., 1958), 108.

THE DEPTH OF JESUS' AGONY ON THE CROSS

"If I only knew." "My God, why?" These are your questions and mine. We have all known some dark night, that sense of forsakenness – being cut off, empty, void, or separated. But no matter how black the dark night of our soul may have been or is, it cannot begin to compare to what our Lord went through on the cross. As deep as the depth of our depression and agony might be, there was a depth in his agony that goes beyond all of our human agony. There are varieties of forsakenness in the human experience, but the mysterious depth of our Lord's abandonment is not on the same level. This scaffold on Calvary—the dreaded Place of the Skull – reached into the heart of the eternal God.

I tremble as I try to speak about this event. I fear attempting to say more than anybody can know. How do you penetrate into the mystery of the great unknown "burden" which Jesus was bearing on the cross? We cannot fathom it. I hesitate to try to explain the unexplainable. "By the standards of the cry of the dying Jesus for God," Jürgen Moltmann observes, "theological systems collapse at once in their inadequacy."[2] We are at the edge of the relationship of the Father and Son. Words are inadequate; nevertheless, we must say something. But we take off our shoes as we stand before a mystery that is beyond our comprehension and beyond our ability to articulate what is happening here. Yet we grope into the dark in an effort to understand it. Here on this cross is the central event of our faith. Here we stand before the mystery of the incarnation and the atonement. How can we grasp their meaning? I shake and shudder to try to explain the unexplainable.

---

2 Jürgen Moltmann, *The Crucified God* (New York: Harper & Row, 1974), 153. See my book *The Church Under the Cross* (Gonzalez, Florida : Energion Publications, 2012) for my more detailed perspective on the meaning of the cross of Jesus.

A CRY OF ABSENCE

Jesus cried: "*Eli, Eli, lama sabachthani*." "My God, my God, why have you forsaken me?" What was this cry? It was a cry of absence. There could be no more isolation than being nailed to a cross. Spikes were driven through his hands and feet. He was impaled on a wooden stake set up by the roadside outside the walls of Jerusalem. It was a time of emptiness, silence, barrenness and void. The hour which he had said was coming had now arrived. "My God, let this cup pass from me if it is possible," he prayed the night before in the Garden of Gethsemane. But it was not. He had to drink it. And now here he was hanging on that cross. His disciples had scattered, but he was there on Golgotha.

WHAT PROVOKED THIS FEELING?

What provoked Jesus' sense of forsaken-ness? Was it the betrayal by Judas, the denial by Peter, or the desertion by all the other disciples? Was it the changing mood of the crowd which had said a week before: "Hallelujah," and today: "Crucify him!"? Was it the physical agony that he endured? Was it the four mock trials before Annas, Caiaphas, Herod, and Pilate? Was it the beating that he had received only a few hours earlier or the physical torture of hanging on the cross for six hours?

Wallace Viets said that he saw a French movie on the crucifixion of Christ several years ago. In this French version rather than showing the actual flogging of Jesus by the Roman soldiers, the camera focused on the faces of the crowd of people who were looking through a small barred window into the courtyard of the dungeon where Jesus was being scourged by the soldiers. At first the faces of the frenzied, hatefilled crowd seemed enthusiastic, and seemed to be enjoying Jesus' beating. As the scourging continues, the expression on their faces slowly changes and they begin to be nauseated and they turn their faces away from the window and begin to be sick.[3]

3   Wallace T. Viets, *My God, Why?* (Nashville: Abingdon Press, 1966), 68.

THE SILENCE OF GOD

Jesus experienced the absence of God. "God, why are you so silent in the face of my suffering?" We can bear almost anything if there is response from those we love. But silence? "0 God, do not keep silence; do not hold your peace and be still, 0 God" (Ps. 83:1). How do you bear the silence of heaven—the absence of God? Martin Marty went through this kind of struggle after the death of his wife. His book, *A Cry of Absence: Reflections from the Winter of the Heart,* expresses his pain.

> Try as I might, I can not make a river of my bed with tears. Whereas others ask, "Is God gracious?" I ask, "Is God?"; does God appear at all? My heaven is not too threatened with the nearness of God. Instead it seems empty and silent. My horizon knows no skyline of the City of God. It only offers more distant horizons.[4]

He too knew a cry of absence.

A CRY OF DERELICTION

"*Eli, Eli, lama sabachthani.*" "My God, my God, why have you forsaken me?" It was a cry of dereliction. It was a cry of forsakenness, desolation and utter aloneness. Had God forsaken his Son? A derelict ship is a ship in which the captain, the crew, compass and cargo are all gone. Nothing is left. Even the rats have abandoned a derelict ship. Jesus' cry of dereliction was his feeling that God had literally abandoned his Son. Jesus cried out: "Where are you? Have you withdrawn your presence from me?"

A WITHDRAWAL OF GOD'S FELLOWSHIP

The pain was even greater for Jesus, because he had experienced an unbroken sense of fellowship with the Father. As a lad

---

4 Martin E. Marty, *A Cry of Absence* (San Francisco: Harper & Row, 1983), 107.

of twelve when Mary and Joseph returned to Jerusalem and found him talking with the rabbis in the temple, he responded: "I must be in my Father's house." He taught his disciples to pray, "Our Father." He had even daringly said, "He that has seen me has seen the Father." "I and the Father are one." He had talked about his relationship to God as "Abba, Father." His fellowship with God was a close communion.

Now, hanging between heaven and earth, suddenly like a lightning flash there was a sense of brokenness, separation, a withdrawal of God. The tense here for forsaken is an *aorist*, which indicates that what was happening here was experienced in this moment. It was not a continuous experience. Jesus felt a withdrawal of the presence that always had sustained him. He was now totally alone. That sacred fellowship and communion with the Father were suspended from him. He had never known this pain of isolation before.

JESUS CRIES TO GOD NOT FATHER

For the first time in these moments we hear rising to the lips of Jesus not the word "Father" for God. This is the only time we ever hear Jesus address God as God and not Father. "My God," he cried. Here on his cross he was hanging with a sense of aloneness – more than a sense – the reality of separation from the Father. It was a cry of dereliction – forsaken. How can we possibly grasp Jesus' sense of forsakenness? We can't. We can only stand at the edge of this great mystery. We probe this mystery but cannot penetrate it.

A CRY OF IDENTIFICATION

"My God, my God, why have you forsaken me?" was also a cry of identification. Here we see Jesus Christ identifying with humanity. Nowhere will you ever see the humanity in Christ demonstrated more vividly than at the cross when he sensed forsakenness. Here we see his full humanity. This is no playacting, no illusion. Here is a man suffering. We see the complete identification of Christ with us. The Apostle Paul, in his letter to the Philippians worded this truth like this in the second chapter: "For the divine nature was his from the first, yet he did not think to snatch at equality with God, but made himself nothing, assuming the nature of a slave. Bearing the human likeness, revealed in human shape, he humbled himself in obedience accepted even death, death on a cross"(Phil. 2:68).

Jesus Identified With Us

At the cross Jesus identified completely with humanity. The Word was flesh. The darkness in this picture symbolizes not only the darkness in the world at that moment – the ninth hour – but the darkness in the heart of God at the sin of humanity. At the cross Jesus was identifying with the sins of humanity. This identification was necessary, not because he had sinned, but because somehow he must experience what sin was. Isaiah had written earlier: "The Lord has laid on him the iniquity of us all" (Isaiah 53:6). Paul, writing to the Corinthians, said: "He that knew no sin was made sin for us" (II Cor. 5:21). Somehow in the awesome mystery of his dying on the cross, Jesus identified with our sins and bore our sins.

A Separation from the Father

What was the effect of Jesus bearing the sins of humanity? Somehow it caused separation of the Son from the Father. Oh, how do you probe this kind of theological mystery? Who can fathom the relationship of the Son and the Father as Jesus was dying on the cross? Since sin separates us from God, somehow in this moment of bearing the sins of humanity, Jesus experienced what that separation was. The Apostle's Creed states that Jesus "descended into hell." What is that symbolism? Hell is separation from God. At the cross Jesus somehow, in this agonizing experience of bearing human sin, knew this separation. As he identified with your sins and my sins, he experienced the bottom of despair—utter desolation. The costly nature of the atonement is revealed here. There is an unbelievable horror to human sinfulness.

Sin tears God apart. The Son was separated from the Father. Jesus bore our sins and guilt in his suffering. Look how our sins tore his heart apart. Look at the wound our sins caused and the blood that was spilled on that cross for you and me. The worst agony of all for him was his separation from the fellowship of his Father.

THE BURDEN OF HUMAN SINS

Helmut Thielicke discusses the Sigmaringen picture of Christ under the title *One Must Watch*, which was depicted by Manfred Hausmann. The scene is the Last Supper, and the disciple John is seen sleeping on Jesus' breast. While John is sleeping peacefully, Christ looks out on the world with a glance of omniscience. We see through the eyes of Jesus what he envisions as he approaches the cross. His look embraces all of the sorrow of the world. He sees the filth and shame in the most secret recesses of the human hearts. He hears the cries of the tortured and those racked by anxiety. He sees the suffering of the animal creation and the smallest woe of the human soul.[5]

Here on Golgotha somehow every agony, every abandoned child, every forsaken mother, every aching father, all of the hurts of humanity, the sins of humanity, are placed on Jesus' back. This burden of sinfulness crushes him down into despair, and he feels forsakenness. Jesus' words are an absolute cry of identification as he bears your sins, my sins, and the sins of all men and women.

A CRY OF EXPECTATION

But then the cry, "My God, my God, why have you forsaken me?" is also a cry of expectation. The words from Jesus are addressed to God. "*My* God, why have *you* forsaken me?" Jesus did not turn *away* from God, but he turned *to* God. He does not fall away from God, but he falls into the arms of God. He turned to God, not the soldiers, religious leaders, disciples, family or the crowd. The fact

---

5   Helmut Thielicke, *The Silence of God* (Grand Rapids, Michigan: William B. Eerdmans Co., 1962), 73-74..

that he addressed his prayer to God is evidence that there was still faith within his heart. This is the only record in the gospels where Jesus addressed a question to God. And it was a prayer.

JESUS DIED BY FAITH LIKE WE HAVE TO

As Jesus was hanging on this cross, his mind in this moment was filled with a mixture of faith and doubt. His humanity was real. I will never forget the time I heard Carlyle Marney speak in chapel when I was a student in seminary. Marney was reflecting on the death of Jesus on the cross. "When Jesus was dying on the cross," Marney declared, "he did not know he would be raised from the grave. He did not know it. He 'faithed' it just like you and I must." If Jesus knew it absolutely, he was not human. He would have been pretending. If he were not human, then the Incarnation was not real. He had to "faith" it just as you and I do when we come to our time of dying. He cast himself, as we must, in trust upon God.

WAS JESUS RECITING PSALM 22?

Others see this cry as one of expectation because they believe Jesus was reciting the 22nd Psalm. This psalm begins with the words: "My God, my God why hast thou forsaken me and art so far from saving me, and heeding my groans? 0 my God, I cry in the day but thou dost not answer, in the night I cry but get no respite" (vv12). Listen to some of the other images: "I am abused by all men, scorned by the people. All who see me jeer at me, make mouths at me and wag their heads: 'He threw himself on the Lord for rescue; let the Lord deliver him, for he holds him dear!'. . My strength drains away like water and all my bones are loose. My heart has turned to wax and melts within me. My mouth is dry as a potsherd, and my tongue sticks to my jaw; I am laid low in the dust of death. The huntsmen are all around me; a band of ruffians ring me round . . . They share out my garments among them and cast lots for my clothes. But do not remain so far away, 0 Lord; 0 my help, hasten to my aid" (vv. 619).

Now listen to the cry of assurance from the latter part of the psalm. "Praise him, you who fear the Lord; all you sons of Jacob, do him honor, stand in awe of him. For he has not scorned the downtrodden, nor shrunk in loathing from his plight, nor hidden his face from him, but gave heed to him when he cried out . . . Let all ends of the earth remember and turn again to the Lord" (vv. 23-24, 26). This psalm ends with a cry of assurance and faith that the God who seemed to be so far away, was, nevertheless, present.

God Was In Christ

Though Jesus did experience a real sense of abandonment here, and in reality there was a withdrawal of God's presence, God could not be nearer than he was at this cross. To deny the presence of God is to deny the Incarnation. Here is the great paradox God had withdrawn, but was at the same time present. "God was in Christ reconciling the world unto himself," Paul wrote (II Cor. 5:19). Here is the mystery of the God who withdrew, but the God who was also present. God was himself involved in the life which was given for you and me that we might have eternal life.

In that beautifully moving novel by Alan Paton, *Cry the Beloved Country*, Kumalo, a black priest, faces the tragedy of his own son being executed for the murder of a white man. He doesn't know how to face his son's death. "Sorrow is better than fear," said Father Vincent, a white priest. "Fear is a journey, a terrible journey, but sorrow is at last an arriving." "And where have I arrived?" asked Kumalo. "No one can comprehend the ways of God," says Father Vincent. Kumalo looked at him, not bitterly or accusingly or reproachfully. "It seems that God has turned away from me," he said. "This may seem to happen," said Father Vincent. "But it does not happen, never, never, does it happen!"[6]

---

6   Alan Paton, *Cry, the Beloved Country* (New York: Charles Scribner's Sons, 1948), 108.

JESUS OVERCAME OUR SEPARATION FROM GOD

This is the victorious shout of the Christian faith. Whatever has happened at this cross reveals the faithfulness of God. In those moments of separation from God which Jesus Christ experienced in his dying, he was able to overcome our separation from God. Because of his sacrifice, you and I are able to experience communion and fellowship with God. The eternal God is faithful. We affirm with confidence that "the Lord is my shepherd and I shall not want." We live with the reassurance that God's presence abides with us always.

The Apostle Paul, writing to the Roman church, gives us a ringing cry of assurance when he says: "Then what can separate us from the love of Christ? Can affliction or hardship? Can persecution, hunger, nakedness, peril, or the sword? We are being done to death for thy sake all day long . . . Yet in spite of all . . . I am convinced that there is nothing in death or life, in the realm of spirit or superhuman powers, in the world as it is or in the world as it shall be, in the forces in the universe, in the heights or the depths nothing in all creation that can separate us from the love of God in Christ Jesus our Lord" (Rom. 8:35-39).

In the death of Jesus Christ on that cross, God has overcome the separation that you and I have experienced because of our sin. You and I, through faith, can experience communion with God which begins in this life and stretches into eternity. May you and I all have a strong awareness of God's presence.

CHAPTER 5

THE HAUNTING VOICE
OF HUMAN NEED

JOHN 19:28-29

The sleep of the couple was interrupted as a voice broke into the night. "Momma, Daddy! I'm thirsty!" he cried. This is a familiar cry to which many parents have responded. Sometimes this cry has arisen out of some physical need; at other times because of a high fever.

"I'm thirsty!" That's not a cry many of us express often. Few of us have really known thirst in our country. Oh, we may have labored long in the hot sun, or engaged in some sports activity, but after a while, we knew we could go over and get a drink of water. There have been travelers across desert regions who ran out of water and would dig like animals under rocks searching for some sign of water. Others of these desert travelers have sometimes seen a mirage—an oasis—off in the distance. One of the last pleas from those who are dying is, "Water." Soldiers have been wounded on the battlefield, and the fighting is so intense that others are unable to reach them. But they still hear their haunting cry, "Water!" Those who have been shipwrecked and set afloat in a small raft have known what thirst is really like. Sometimes these shipwrecked persons have become so crazed by the sun that they have reached down and have drunk from the salt water. They were unable to restrain themselves any longer.

No, if we are honest, most of us have never really experienced thirst at all. But the ancient people in Israel knew something about thirst. They lived all of their lives on the edge of a desert, and the first greeting a person often made to someone when they met was: "Would you like some water?"

Crucifixion was meant to be ugly and nasty. Jesus was nailed to a cross outside the Jerusalem walls like a common criminal. It was a horrible experience. One of the worst parts of that experience was the agony of dying of thirst. The Romans wanted this way of putting criminals to death to be a horrible experience. Their cruel death was to serve as an example to deter any other criminals. You remember Jesus' pilgrimage to the cross after his prayer that he might avoid this cup in the Garden of Gethsemane. He was betrayed, arrested on the Mount of Olives, went through several mock trials, was scourged and had to bear his cross to the Place of the Skull outside the city gates. There he was laid on a wooden cross and spikes were driven through his hands and feet. He was lifted up on his cross and placed between two criminals to die.

As we have examined his last words on the cross to this point, we have heard Jesus pray for his enemies as he said: "Father, forgive them, for they know not what they do." Then he extended his promise to the dying criminal nearby, who asked, "Lord, remember me when you come into your kingdom." Jesus responded by saying: "This day you will be with me in Paradise." The next words expressed his compassion for his mother as he directed John to care for her, and for her to look upon John as her own son. The last word we looked at was Jesus' cry of desertion, "My God, why have you forsaken me?"

We come to examine the fifth word, "I thirst." In English it is two words, but in Greek it is only one. These words were the shortest of all his sayings on the cross. "I thirst." Let's see if we can capture something of what these words might mean.

THE HUMANITY OF JESUS

To begin with, it seems to me that these words are clearly evident of the humanity of Jesus. Jesus was hanging on that cross. His body was bleeding, aching, and racked with fever and pain. After hanging on his cross for about six hours in the hot sun, he cried out: "I thirst!" This was a sign of the physical suffering of Jesus.

The earliest Christian heresy was not about the divinity of Jesus, but was a denial that Jesus was really human. The Docetics taught that Jesus just pretended to be a man. The advocates of this philosophy about Jesus said that Jesus did not even leave footprints when he walked. He did not have a real body and only playacted that he was a man. John's gospel thrusts the humanity of Jesus clearly before his readers in the words. "And the word became flesh and dwelt among us" (John 1:14).

THE DISCIPLES SAW JESUS' HUMANITY

The disciples knew the humanity of Jesus. They had witnessed it daily. They started following Jesus not because they first perceived of him as divinely related to God. Oh, no. They saw him as a rabbi, a teacher. They saw him when he was frustrated. They heard him exclaim: "Why can't you watch with me one hour?" They witnessed his anger as he kicked over the tables of the moneychangers in the temple. They saw him sorrowful as he wept by the grave of his friend Lazarus. They saw him get hungry, tired, and thirsty. They knew that he was a human being. "Whenever we emphasize the divinity of Jesus at the expense of his humanity," Marcus Borg asserts, "we lose track of the utterly remarkable human being that he was."[1]

Michelangelo's Pieta shows a shrunken Jesus whom Mary held in her arms after the crucifixion. The symbolism of this sculpture by Michelangelo was that something physical happened to Jesus on the cross. His pain, anguish, and death were real.

JESUS IDENTIFIED WITH OUR THIRST

On the cross Jesus identified with the thirst of humanity. His thirst was an identification with the thirst that every person has.

---

1   Marcus J. Borg, *The Heart of Christianity* (New York: HarperOne, 2004), 83.

The human thirst is not limited, however, to the physical. There is a thirst for love, and the thirst for acceptance, recognition, hope, meaning, and purpose in life.

In one of the *Peanuts* comic strips, Charlie Brown was seen talking to a friend. "When Grandpa was small," he said, "the doctor gave him baby aspirin. He went to the cardiologist recently and he told him to take a baby aspirin each day. Grandpa says he is not sure he is getting anyplace." There are a lot of folks in life who feel at times that they are not getting anyplace in life. Their longings, gropings, hungers, and thirsting are never satisfied.

When Jesus cried out, "I thirst," it was an identification with the thirst of every person. Whatever fevered brow you have experienced, whatever pain you have known, whatever hardship or physical burden you have borne, be assured that here at this cross Jesus has identified with you. His suffering is his identification with the suffering of humanity everywhere. Later Peter would write, "Cast all of your cares upon him, because he cares for you" (I Peter 5:7).

When John Claypool was pastor of Crescent Hill Baptist Church in Louisville, Kentucky his nine year old daughter was diagnosed with leukemia. She asked her father one day, "Daddy, have you prayed to God about my illness?" "Yes, honey," he said, "I've prayed." "Well, what did he say? "she asked.

That is the cry of many of us in the face of our suffering. The response that comes to us from God is always that God knows, understands, senses, and feels our pain. God is there with us in the midst of our suffering. Nothing separates us from God's love. Christ identifies with us. Christ knows the weight of our pain because he too was human.

A Spiritual Thirst

There is possibly a deeper meaning in Jesus' thirst. I think there may be more here than physical thirst. I think his thirst was physical. Yes, it was very physical indeed. But I think there was another dimension to his suffering. There may have been a spiritual depth to this thirst. Jesus' words may have echoed the sixtythird Psalm. In the sixtythird Psalm the writer cried: "Oh, God, you are my God. I long for you. My whole being desires you, like a dry, wornout and waterless land, my soul is thirsty for you" (Ps. 63:1). There was a thirst for God.

Was there not somehow in the cry of Jesus a sense of thirst for the living water he had experienced with his Father? I wrote earlier about the forsakenness which Jesus felt when he bore the sins of humanity. He had already felt forsaken by God. He underwent isolation from his Father. This spiritual thirst was necessary for him to experience the burden of humanity. In the Apostles' Creed it states, "He descended into hell."

When Jesus bore in his death the burden of our sinfulness, it separated him from God's presence. In this moment of his physical thirst there was also a haunting spiritual cry, "I thirst for God's presence." "My throat is as dry as dust, and my tongue sticks to the roof of my mouth. You have left me for dead in the dust" (Ps. 22: 15). That's physical thirst.

Psalm 42 reads, "As a deer longs for the flowing streams, so longs my soul for thee, O God. My soul thirsts for God, for the living God. When shall I become and behold the face of God? My tears have been my food day and night, while men say to me continually, 'Where is your God?'" (Ps. 42:14). That's spiritual thirst. The irony in Jesus' cry is that the One who said that he would give us living water—his presence would be like a flowing fountain of water—he himself had to experience the thirst of every human soul before he could quench our thirst. He had to know what our thirst was like.

BEARING HUMAN SIN

Jesus' thirst might be a metaphor for the burden of bearing human sin. In one of the parables of Jesus, he speaks about the rich man and Lazarus. In this parable Jesus told about the rich man

who was in hell and cried out: "Father Abraham, send Lazarus
that he might dip his finger in water and cool my tongue because
I am in torment." Separation from God brings a thirst that cannot
be satisfied apart from the presence of God. Our soul hungers and
thirsts for that satisfaction. Maybe this cry of Jesus was the desire
to have the union with his Father restored. It had been broken by
the burden of sin that he had to bear, and he longed once again to
have the fellowship that he had enjoyed so much.

A Roman soldier took a sponge and dipped it in common wine
and touched it to Jesus' lips to satisfy his thirst. In John's image that
sponge was extended on a stick of hyssop. Hyssop was the small
bush that was used to smear blood on the door post of the Israelites'
houses in Egypt when the angel of death passed over their house.
Hyssop in this image from John symbolizes the Paschal Lamb, the
Passover Lamb. John saw Jesus' death as the Lamb of God.

In the central stained glass window behind the pulpit in St.
Matthews Baptist Church, Louisville, Kentucky is a picture of a
slain lamb on a cross. This image is Jesus as the Lamb of God who
takes away the sins of the world.

A RESPONSE TO JESUS' CRY

Notice the response to Jesus' cry. A soldier lifted up a sponge
to Jesus to satisfy that thirst. When Jesus first arrived at the place
to be crucified, the soldiers tried to give him some wine which
was mixed with myrrh as a narcotic to dull the pain. But Jesus rejected this wine. The feet of Jesus on the cross were probably only
about eighteen inches off the ground. The soldiers could likely have
reached the cup to him. It would have been awkward, however,
to try to give him something to drink. The soldier put wine on a
sponge and reached up to Jesus' lips with it.

Mark states that the soldier did this to mock Jesus. He gave
him vinegar, not satisfying wine. There are a lot of us who give Jesus
vinegar to drink when he cries out to us, don't we? When we need

to take a stand for him at school or at work or when we face temptations, we give him vinegar instead of a life that testifies to him.

But I think the other gospels record the proper emphasis. A soldier had likely brought a lunch with him that day with a common flask of wine. Many soldiers would bring this cheap wine with them. He then poured some of his wine on a sponge and out of kindness offered it to Jesus. He did this to help our Lord in the midst of his suffering. We don't know what this soldier's name was. I am sure few soldiers ever did any act of kindness to someone who was dying from being crucified. But this one did. Our Lord still has a thirst which is expressed in the thirst of others in the world today. Would you – will you – respond today?

I love that old story that took place in the Armargosa desert where Desert Pete, as he was called, left a note in an old baking soda can which he tied to a pump in the middle of the desert. As travelers eighty years ago would come that way, they would reach in that baking soda can and pull out the following note:

> This pump is all right as of June, 1932. I put a new sucker washer into it and it ought to last five years. But the washer dries out and the pump has got to be primed. Under the white rock I buried a bottle of water, out of the sun and cork end up. There's enough water in it to prime the pump, but not if you drink some first. Pour about one fourth and let her soak to wet the leather. Then pour in the rest medium fast and pump like crazy. You'll git water. The well has never run dry. Have faith. When you git watered up, fill the bottle and put it back like you found it for the next feller. (signed) Desert Pete.
> P.S. Don't go drinking up the water first. Prime the pump with it and you'll git all you can hold.

THE THIRSTY AROUND US

Life is like that, too, you know. There are people all around us who are thirsty, and they are extending their cups to us. If we try to drink all of the "water" we have received from Christ for ourselves, we will never be able to help them. We have got to be willing to pour some water into their cups to satisfy their thirst.

Do you remember the words from Jesus where he said, "Inasmuch as you have done it unto the least of these you have done it unto me?" "Lord, when did we give somebody a cup of cold water?" When someone else was thirsty and you extended water to them, you gave water to Christ. Jesus began his ministry in Samaria by speaking to a woman at the well. He asked her: "Give me a drink of water." Then on the cross as he was dying he cried, "I thirst."

THE LIVING WATER

The great message from John is that the One who had asked for water is himself the living fountain who can furnish water to anyone who is thirsty. You and I, who have drunk from this fountain, are now asked to reach out into the world and share with others the water that we have experienced in Christ. We share the water that has quenched our thirst.

In his journey across the wilderness, Moses tapped a rock in the desert and God caused a spring of water to pour from it. It is that analogy that Christina Rossetti draws upon in these words:

> Am I a stone and not a sheep
> That I can stand, O Christ, beneath Thy Cross
> To number drop by drop Thy Blood's slow loss,
> And yet not weep?
> Not so those women loved
> Who with exceeding grief lamented Thee;
> Not so fallen Peter weeping bitterly;
> Not so the thief was moved;
> Not so the sun and moon
> Which hid their faces in a starless sky,
> A horror of great darkness at broad noon
> I, only I.
> Yet give not o'er,

But seek Thy sheep, true Shepherd of the flock,
Greater than Moses,
turn and look once more
And smite a rock.[2]

May God smite us who have become unmoving and rocklike in our concern for him and others. May he smite us so we, too, might let his water flow from us. May we draw water once again from Christ, who is the living fountain of God.

O God, we do thirst. We thirst so for your Spirit. Satisfy that desire by the cooling, quenching love of your grace. O God, we know we drop the ball so often as we look around us and do not fill the cups that are extended to us for your love and grace. Smite us, O God, and teach us how to care. Through Christ who loves us so much that he laid down his life for us, we pray. Amen.

---

2 Christina Rossetti, "Good Friday," in *Masterpieces of Religious Verse,* edited by James Dalton Morrison (New York: Harper and Brothers Publishers, 1948), 186.

CHAPTER 6

THE TRIUMPHANT SHOUT

JOHN 19:30

For six hours Jesus had hung upon the cross. He seemed to realize that the end was near, and with a loud shout he cried: "It is finished!" But what was finished? The religious authorities had finished their accusations. The political authorities had finished their condemnation. The mob had finished their jeers and cries of "Crucify Him!" The soldiers had finished their nasty job of nailing him to that wooden tree. Yes, these persons had finished their work.

WHAT WAS FINISHED?

But what did Jesus mean, "It is finished?" Were these words merely indicating that he realized that the physical end of his life was near; that everything that he had hoped for and dreamed for was not going to be realized? Was he feeling that his life was over, defeated, all was lost, and he was at the end of his rope?

WHO FINISHES ANYTHING?

But who really finishes anything? If you stop and think about it, very few of us could ever say, "I have finished what I want to do in life." I have talked with many elderly persons who knew that they were close to the end of their life, and I will be honest with you, I have never had anyone say to me, "I have finished or accomplished all I wanted to do in my life." Most of them still have much they want to do. It may be as simple as seeing a grandchild get married or a child or grandchild graduate from school, or it may be some other task at home or with their work or avocation that they still want to realize.

When Michelangelo died, his students discovered many unbelievable goals that he had lined out in front of him to do. When A. M. Fairbairn, who had been principal at Mansfield College in Oxford died in his late eighties, his family said that he had left manuscripts and other documents which outlined work that he wanted to do which would have taken another person a hundred years to accomplish. Most of us will never say, "I have reached the point where I have finished everything."

A VICTORY CRY

Yet Jesus cried, "It is finished." It was not a cry of resignation, however. The other gospels indicate that there was a great shout before Jesus died. They do not indicate what it was. But John does. The loud cry was, "It is finished." The Greek word is translated in the New English Bible as "It is accomplished." The words ring with the idea of a soldier who had fulfilled his mission. For Jesus the cry, "It is finished," was a shout of triumph. *Tetelastai,* "It is accomplished," is a victory cry.

LIFE AS IT WAS MEANT TO BE

What had Jesus finished? Well, for one thing, he had finished living life as it was meant to be lived. We see in Jesus Christ the life of one who was in perfect communion with the Father. He lived the kind of life that God has called all of us to have.

At the beginning of his ministry, Jesus faced the temptation to corrupt God's will for his life. He was tempted to turn stones into bread and to win people to him by economic means. The second temptation he faced was to jump off the pinnacle of the temple. This was the temptation to win people by entertainment. He was tempted to turn religion into a show and make it a circus.

The third temptation was to worship Satan's power. All the kingdoms of the earth would be his. This was the temptation to use military and political power to achieve his ends. These are the temptations before all leaders. He was tempted to use economic, entertainment, military and political power to bring in God's kingdom. Unfortunately, too many religious leaders have utilized the very temptations which Jesus rejected.

Jesus emptied himself of any personal desires and opened himself completely to draw others only to the Father. He was Adam as Adam was created to be. Jesus lived in communion and fellowship with God. He was man with a capital M, man who was Man or better put, man who was fully identified as a human being. In his life was manifested the incarnate Son of God. "The word became flesh." He lived life in perfect communion with the Father. He lived life in complete openness and responsiveness to God.

JESUS REVEALED THE WAY OF LIFE

Secondly, Jesus disclosed the way of life. He said, "I have come that you might have life and have it more abundantly" (John 10:10). "I am the way, the truth, and the life" (John 14:6). In the life of Jesus Christ, in his teachings, in his example everything he said and did disclosed how persons are to live and relate to each other and to God, and how one understands himself or herself fully. He disclosed to us the way of real living.

Jesus did not tell his followers; "I am going to leave you some instructions on how to live," as good as the Beatitudes and his other teachings were. He didn't say that he would draw a map for his followers. He said, "I am the way." He calls us to follow him. He gave us more than words. He gave his life and his dying for us. His life, death, and resurrection are all intertwined with what he taught. We can't really understand the golden rule or the Beatitudes if we do not kneel before the Master who taught them. Jesus has disclosed to us that the real way of life is lived in fellowship with the Father and in a life of service for him.

THE NATURE OF GOD

Third, Jesus had finished revealing to us what the nature of God was like. John writes in another place, "No one has seen God. Only the son who was in the bosom of the Father has made him known" (John 1:18). Jesus was bold to declare, "He that hath seen me has seen the Father" (John 14:9). Why do we ask for some other sign about God? The central sign was in Jesus Christ. "He that hath seen me," Jesus said, "has seen the Father." The cross that was planted on that hillside centuries ago disclosed the nature of God. Jesus revealed that in God's heart was redemptive, suffering love. Jesus was the lamb that was slain from the foundation of the world.

In Jesus Christ we see revealed what God is like. God is a God of love, not vindictiveness and hate. Jesus revealed a God of compassion and mercy, a God that reaches out to embrace all persons with love and mercy. The neurosurgeon, Dr. Eben Alexander, declared that his "near-death experience" taught him that God's love is unconditional. "Love is without doubt," Alexander stated, "the basis of everything." This love," he continues "is the reality of realities, the incomprehensibly glorious truth of truths that lives and breathes at the core of everything that exists or will exist, and no remotely accurate understanding of who and what we are can be achieved by anyone who does not know it, and embody it in all of their actions."[1] Having seen the depth of God's love in Christ, the Christian is challenged to live out that love in his or her life.

The life, death, and resurrection of Christ are like a chip into a tree. We see inside the tree from that chip and discover something about the nature of that tree. When a volcano has ripped open the earth, we are able to see through that crack into the fiery depths of the earth. We see into the center of the earth in a way we never could before.

---

1 Eben Alexander, *Proof of Heaven: A Neurosurgeon's Journey into the Afterlife* (New York: Simon & Schuster, 2012), 71.

In the life, death, and resurrection of Christ, we see something about the nature of God. And what has been revealed to us is that God is a God of love, understanding, and mercy.

JESUS FINISHED THE WORK OF REDEMPTION

Fourth, Jesus has finished the work of redemption. The Old Testament is filled with prophesies about the One who was to come as a Savior, where he would be born, the name of the town, the fact that his mother would be a virgin, and that he would be bruised for our iniquity, and on him the chastisement of our sins would be laid. Jesus fulfilled the prophesy about the One who would be the lamb, lion, the king, the shepherd, and the ruler of Israel. He fulfilled the Old Testament prophesies that pointed men and women to the Messiah who was to come.

Jesus made the message clear about why he came. He said, "I have come to seek and to save those who are lost. The whole don't need a physician but those who are sick do" (Luke 19:10). He came to bring balm to sinners. He was the Lamb of God. He was the Paschal Lamb, about whom John wrote, that was crucified at twelve o'clock noon the same hour the Paschal Lamb was sacrificed in the temple. Christ was crucified at that moment as God's Passover Lamb. But Jesus was more than just the Lamb, he was also the Shepherd. Jesus said, "Greater love has no man than he lay down his life for his friends" (John 15:13). "I lay down my life for the sheep" (John 10:15). Jesus was the Shepherd who was willing to sacrifice his life that you and I might have life.

DIRECT ACCESS TO GOD

Through the redeeming work of Jesus' death, the veil of the temple was torn in half. This curtain of blue, purple, and scarlet color had separated men and women from the holy of holies and the mystery of God's presence. Persons had to approach God through a high priest and use sacrificial animals to express the symbolism of their worship. Through the death of Christ this veil was torn asunder. Persons can go directly into God's presence because Jesus has made that access possible. Jesus was the Lamb and the sacrifice. The work of redemption was complete in his death. That is what he has finished. He has finished the atoning work. Because of his atoning death, you and I as sinners can experience forgiveness from God.

AN UNFINISHED DIMENSION OF JESUS' DEATH

Notice that there is an unfinished dimension to Jesus' death. Christ has finished his work, but for us there is an unfinished part. The unfinished part of Christ's death is what is your responsibility and my responsibility now. Jesus has finished his part, but now as you and I receive this redemption, we are called upon to be agents of reconciliation, to share God's love with other people. Having received such grace, we now are commanded to tell others about this grace. Jesus founded the Church but you and I are called to continue building it.

Jesus has given the cup of salvation through his death, but you and I must accept it and drink it to receive redemption. Jesus stands at the door and knocks, but you and I must open the door. He commands us to go and tell others, but you and I must respond. Yes, there is an unfinished dimension to the work of Christ. You and I are called upon to tell others of God's finished work in Christ so they too can share in his wonderful, redeeming grace. "The cross of Jesus is thus the Christian symbol par excellence," N. T. Wright declares, "forming the focal point of Christian spirituality, Christian praying, Christian believing, and Christian action."[2]

H. Wheeler Robinson, the Old Testament Baptist scholar, said that one day a French skeptic wandered into a Paris cathedral during the singing of the twentythird portion of the Mass which begins, "*Agnus Dei, qui tollis peccata, mundi, misere nobis.*" "Lamb of God, who takes away the sin of the world, have mercy upon

2   Marcus J. Borg and N. T. Wright, *The Meaning of Jesus: Two Visions* (San Francisco: Harper Collins Paperback, 2000), 107.

us." Touched by the wonder of these words, the skeptic cried, "The Lamb of God! If only he could! What a dream!"

But that's the gospel! "The Lamb of God who takes away the sin of the world. Lord, have mercy!" That is what has been finished. Jesus' death was God's great act of atonement. He invites you and me to respond to this love. It is indeed amazing grace.

Gustaf Aulén, the Swedish theologian, affirms the victory which Christ won in his struggle with the powers of evil. He calls us back to the classic idea of the Atonement which asserts that:

> . . . the Atonement is, above all, a movement of God to man, not in the first place a movement of man to God. We shall hear again its tremendous paradoxes: that God, the all-ruler, the Infinite, yet accepts the lowliness of the Incarnation; we shall hear again the old realistic message of the conflict of God with the dark, hostile forces of evil, and His victory over them by the Divine self sacrifice; above all, we shall hear again the note of triumph.
>
> For my own part, I am persuaded that no form of Christian teaching has any future before it except such as it can keep steadily in view the reality of the evil in the world, and go to meet the evil with a battle-song of triumph. Therefore, I believe that the classic idea of the Atonement and of Christianity is coming back—that is to say, the genuine, authentic Christian faith.[3]

In a real engagement with the forces of evil, the One in whom goodness was seen at its highest encountered evil at its worst, and Christ was victorious. The cross seemed a victory for the powers of evil but it was not. Jesus did not say, "I am finished," but "It is finished!" "It is accomplished!" It was a cry of victory. He had met the ultimate powers of evil on the cross and the resurrection affirmed the victory which Jesus won on that wooden cross outside the Jerusalem walls. He was indeed *Christus Victor.*

---

3   Gustaf Aulén, *Christus Victor* (New York: The MacMillan Co., 1958), 159.

CHAPTER 7

THE PRAYER OF TRUST

LUKE 23:44-46

In the previous chapters we have been examining the last words of Jesus on the cross before he died. Each of these words, in a way, is like the string on a musical instrument. Each word sounded a different note which gave insight into the feelings and mind of Jesus as he was dying. We notice, for example, that the first word was one of forgiveness— intercession for his enemies. "Father, forgive them for they know not what they do." The second word was one of assurance, as he said to the thief: "This day you will be with me in Paradise."

The third word was one of guardianship where Jesus voiced his sense of responsibility for his mother before he died. Jesus likely nodded to his mother and John as he said: "Mother, behold your son; and Son, behold your mother." The fourth word was a word of desolation—a sense of forsaken-ness when the burden of sin was so heavy upon his back. The fifth word, "I thirst!" was his physical identification with our own humanity. The sixth word, "It is finished!" was a sense of the completion of the work of redemption.

ABSOLUTE TRUST

We come now to examine the final word. The final words of Jesus were: "Father, into your hands I commit my spirit." These words were a surrender of his life in absolute trust to his Father. One of the things we need to remember as we reflect on Jesus' death on the cross is that his death was not a passive event. Jesus did not simply give up his life and respond as a recipient to the actions of others. Now granted, in a real sense his life was taken. But the gospel writers are adamant in affirming that his death was a life given. There is a paradox here. Jesus was not just a victim, but a victor. He didn't surrender his life but gave it as a sacrifice. Crucifixion was indeed a ghastly act. Nevertheless, the New Testament focuses not on the horror, but on Jesus, as a free act of his will, voluntarily laying down his life for others (John 10:18). John says that Jesus *"gave up* his spirit." His death was depicted as a life given, not just a life taken.

Much of the ancient art depicts Jesus with a crown on his head as he hangs on the cross. There was something victorious in his death. He was reigning from the cross. He was a crowned king, not a defeated rebel (Col. 2:14-15). The final words of Jesus reveal something of that note of victory.

A Prayer to His Father

Jesus said, "Father, into your hands I commit my spirit." This is first of all a prayer. Jesus' first words were a prayer of forgiveness for his enemies. "Father, forgive them for they know not what they do." His words about feeling forsaken were a prayer. The last words on his lips were also a prayer. Prayer had been such a vital part of Jesus' life. Everything he did and said was saturated in prayer.

Jesus began by directing his prayer to his Father. Jesus lifted the word, Father, to a height that persons had never known before. Jesus was not the first person to address God as Father, but he did breathe new meaning and content into it. Even the pagan religions had their fathergods. In Greek mythology Zeus was the father of the gods. Jupiter was the father of the Roman gods in Roman mythology. In these usages the divine father was merely the name of the head of the highest rank in a whole chain of other gods. In the Old Testament God was often spoken of as Father by Israel. But he was depicted as Father in the sense that he had adopted Israel as his nation. His act of adoption had demanded an obedient response from Israel, and only those who were obedient to God were truly his children (Ex. 4:22; Ps. 103:13).

T. W. Manson, the great English New Testament scholar, said that Jesus rarely spoke in public of God as Father but considered the fatherhood of God so sacred that it was reserved for his disciples who would understand. Father was not an image he used broadly about God, because people could not always understand it.[1] But Jesus pushed this image even further and used an expression about God which to many Jewish minds may have appeared disrespectful. In a prayer in Mark 14:36 he used a radically new and different word to describe God with the Aramaic word, "Abba." This Aramaic word was so untranslatable that the early church has preserved the original Aramaic word. The closest possible translation would probably be "daddy." Jesus' sense of the fatherhood of God was a very intimate, personal relationship. After Jesus was crucified, three days later his Father raised him up from the grave. Then forty days later Jesus ascended to sit at the right hand of his Father.

A PRAYER FROM THE SCRIPTURES

Note also that this prayer is drawn from the Scriptures. It was most likely a quotation from Psalm 31:5. Jesus had quoted earlier during his sense of forsakenness from Psalm 22. The Psalms were the hymnbook of Israel. Their words were a part of his whole being. He had absorbed the Psalms and other Scriptures into the deep recesses of his mind.

Earlier in Jesus' life in the time of temptations, when he taught his disciples, confronted the Scribes and Pharisees or others, he would quote Scripture or ask, "Have you not read?" Here in his final moments of dying, Jesus reached back into his mind and drew on that familiar passage of Scripture. Scholars tell us that this passage of Scripture was a part of the ritual that families used at

---

1 T. W. Manson, *The Teaching of Jesus* (Cambridge: Cambridge University Press, 1963), 93ff. See also C. F. D. Moule, "God. NT," *The Interpreters Dictionary of the Bible*, edited by George Arthur Buttrick (New York: Abingdon Press, 1962), 430ff.

their prayers as they gathered together at night before they retired to sleep. The last words they would say were: "Into your hands I commit my spirit." As Jesus was hanging on the cross before he breathed his last, he added the word "Father" to that quotation and prayed: "Father, into your hands I commit my spirit."

A LIFE OF COMMITMENT

Jesus' last words reflect the way he had lived a life of faith and commitment. Jesus didn't just teach about faith. He lived a life of commitment. As a young lad of twelve, he told his parents in the temple, "I must be about my Father's business." "It is my meat," he said, "to do the will of Him who sent me." He left the carpenter's shop, not having any other source of income, and went forth by faith to serve God and preach in the highways, byways and hedges of life, heralding that the kingdom was at hand. He had no place to lay his head but he trusted his Father. He set his face toward Jerusalem. In the Garden of Gethsemane, he prayed, "Not my will but thine be done." He had no place to lay his head but he lived a life of faith and trust in his Father. In the words he said, in his reactions to people, and even in the way he died, he lived what he had taught.

DYING AS HE LIVED

Most people when they come to their time of dying, die as they have lived. Unless their death is sudden, most persons die the same way and with the same kind of personality they have had all along. If a person has had a sense of humor when he or she has been in good health, I have noticed that as long as he or she is conscious and to some degree free of severe pain, that person's humor and personality is basically the same, unless that individual has had a stroke or some debilitating disease that has totally changed his or her personality.

Edwin McNeill Poteat was a noted minister, whose father had also been a minister. His father had been ill for some time and slowly began to realize that he would not live very long. He called Edwin to his bedside and told him that he knew that he was close to the sunset. He then asked his son to conduct his funeral service. "I realize that I am giving you a rather difficult assignment. But, if you will conduct my service this time," he said with a twinkle in his eye, "I promise never to ask you to do it again."

Poteat died as he had lived. He was a man who always had a sense of humor in his life. Even when he approached his time of dying, that humor was not snatched away. Our Lord lived out his trust throughout his life, and when he knew that he was facing death, he reflected that same kind of trust in his dying.

COMMITMENT IS OUR ENTRANCE INTO GOD'S KINGDOM

For you and me commitment is also our entrance into the kingdom of God. We enter the kingdom of Christ through the door of commitment. The gate is narrow. It is the way of surrender, trust and obedience. Jesus called to the disciples by the Sea of Galilee: "Come, follow me."

To Matthew, at the tax collector's desk, Jesus said, "Come follow me." Jesus had told the rich young ruler, "Go and sell all that you have and come follow me." But he refused to make that costly commitment. When Paul met Jesus on the Damascus Road, Paul's life was turned around, and he began to follow Jesus. All of these persons came into the Christian way by an act of commitment. You and I also enter the kingdom of God by an act of faith as we trust Christ.

COMMITMENT AS A WAY OF LIFE

Not only do we enter God's kingdom through trust and surrender, commitment is a way of life for the Christian. The Christian way is a life of faith. We walk onto the bridge of faith, over the chasm of the unknown world before us, and as we walk out upon that bridge, we lean in trust upon God. Paul said, "I was not disobedient to the heavenly vision." (Acts 26:19) "I am crucified with Christ, nevertheless I live, yet not I but Christ lives in me" (Gal. 2:20). "I am persuaded that he is able to keep that which I have committed unto him." (2 Tim. 1:12) The Christian is called to the life of faith as he or she follows the Christ who said, "Take up your cross and follow me." (Mark 8:34) We do not understand everything about the Christian life, but we follow our Lord, who has called us into discipleship.

What a wonderful prayer it would be to begin each day by praying: "Father, into your hands I commit my spirit." This is a prayer not just for the time of dying, but for every day that lies before us. Let us pray:

"Father, into your hands I commit my spirit" as we face the struggles of everyday. Let this be our prayer as we face a new job, begin study in school, meet opportunities for service, confront illness, tragedies, grief, difficulties, a move, or celebrate the birth of a child. Whatever comes our way, we face it with the assurance of God's presence, because we have prayed, "Father, into your hands I commit my spirit."

John Killinger tells about a woman who went to see her ophthalmologist because her eyesight was getting worse. He tried to fit her with glasses to sharpen her images, but he could not. Her eyesight was too poor. But she did not seem too concerned. She told him about her experiences with her family, her husband, and her church. She spoke about the wonderful desires that she felt God had for her. Her doctor observed, "Your eyesight is poor, but your vision is better than perfect."

Jesus Christ gives that gift to all of us who commit our lives to him. Our eyesight, our hearing, our physical conditions may fail, but when we have committed our lives to him, we can live in a trustful way, because we have indeed prayed: "Father, into your hands I commit my spirit." We rest in the spirit of God; lean back in trust upon him and know that he will sustain us.

LIVE AND DIE WITH CONFIDENCE

Then finally we observe that Jesus' words indicate that he died with confidence. Jesus had lived his life with the confidence of God's presence. He had lived his life with a strong sense that God was always with him. When he was a lad of only twelve in the temple, he said he had to be about his Father's business. He was in charge at the wedding in Cana of Galilee where he performed his first miracle. When he began his ministry, when he was tempted and when he faced misunderstanding and rejection, he had confidence that he was doing God's will. When he reached out to minister to those who were suffering, the blind, lame, deaf — he always had a sense of confidence in the power of God with him. With great assurance he stood before the tomb of Lazarus who had been dead three days and cried, "Lazarus, come forth." Jesus declared to his disciples: "I have come that you might have life."

When Jesus came to the last hours of his own life, he maintained his confidence. Jesus stood before Pilate, who was indecisive and had no confidence in his decision. He washed his hands of the matter. Jesus stood before the Sanhedrin where they acted hastily and even violated their own Jewish law in dealing with him. The mob became hysterical and wanted quick solutions. Quietly and confidently Jesus faced what was before him in his trials and crucifixion.

Jesus had prayed in the Garden of Gethsemane that God's will would be done in his life. He accepted the cup of suffering and refused the drug when it was offered to him at the cross so that some of his pain might be abated. While he was hanging nailed to that cross, he forgave his enemies, assured a dying thief that he would be with him in Paradise, and also remembered his mother's future needs. There was a quiet sense of confidence about him throughout all of his life and also in his final moments of dying.

What Is Spirit?

Jesus prayed: "Father, into your hands I commit my spirit." What is spirit? Spirit is the seed that matures into the flower that grows inside the human body. Spirit is the essence of what constitutes the authentic person. The spirit is the mind that is encased in the brain inside our body. What is spirit? It is whatever it is that makes us a personality. It is the real you and me.

I think Paul was writing about this spirit in his letter to the Corinthians when he said that the "perishable nature must put on imperishable, the physical body is raised a spiritual body, and the mortal nature must put on immortality" (I Cor. 15:53). Jesus committed his spirit—what constituted the essence of his personality to his Father. He surrendered what was his true self. "I commit the true me—my spirit—into your hands, Father."

Going Home

Jesus knew that he was going home. Later he told his disciples, "I am going to prepare a place for you." He was going home to his father, and he went with confidence and assurance. I have heard others speak about death as "a going home." When the waves of the storms around you beat against the frail boat of your life, sail on with faith in the Lord of life. He is present with you. Take courage in his presence and know that he will take you home through the storms.

The Scriptures tell us that Jesus bowed his head. That phrase is an image like a child putting his head gently on his pillow at night to go to sleep. Jesus bowed his head. He leaned his head back upon that cross and died with assurance like a child who falls asleep in his father's arms.

"Father, into your hands I commit my spirit." Later these words would be quoted before they died by persons like Charlemagne, Thomas A. Becket, and John Hus as he was being burned at the stake, Martin Luther, Mary, Queen of Scots. John Knox and a host of others. These persons died with these words on their lips:

"Father, I commit my spirit into your hands." What a marvelous prayer by which to live and die.

TRUST NOT ANSWERS

Henry Sloan Coffin, who for many years was president of Union Theological Seminary, in New York City, wrote in a book entitled, *The Meaning of the Cross,* these powerful words:

> We have no explanations to offer perplexed souls in many of the circumstances which raise the insistent, Why? But we have a Figure to set before them, a Fellow sufferer, who dies with an unanswered question on His lips, yet dies placing Himself in his Father's hands. That Figure throughout the Christian centuries has riveted the attention of men (and women) in their most tragic experiences. They looked to Him and find final sympathy, and through Him they regain faith.[2]

We will never have all of the answers to the "whys" or questions about suffering and pain, grief and death. But we look at the figure of Jesus Christ hanging on the cross, knowing that he suffered there for you and me, and as we look at him, we affirm that God was in Christ, and our faith is strengthened and we are sustained by the sense of the presence of God in our own lives. When Fred Craddock was once asked what he thought the people in his Cherry Log Church in Georgia thought he preached, he replied: "I hope they will say: 'He preached that God is one who is kind to the ungrateful and even to the wicked.'"[3] Let us affirm the unconditional love of God which we saw in the sacrificial life and death of Jesus and face death with calm assurance in that grace and love. Harold S. Kushner reminds us that a believer "does not expect God to change things, to eliminate evil, to make his problems disappear.

---

2 Henry Sloane Coffin, *The Meaning of the Cross* (New York: Charles Scribner's Sons, 1959), 95.

3 Fred Craddock, *Craddock on the Craft of Preaching,* edited by Lee Sparks & Kathryn Hayes Sparks (St. Louis, Missouri: Chalice Press, 2011.), 145.

It is enough to believe that God is there for him. Then he knows he is not alone. He knows he has not been abandoned."[4]

Robert Bolt has a magnificent play entitled, "A Man for All Seasons." It is about Sir Thomas Moore, who was willing to die rather than renounce his faith and recognize Henry the Eighth as the supreme head of the Church of England. As he was being led out to be beheaded, his daughter rushed up to him and simply pronounced his name, "Father, Father," as though the pronouncing of his name might somehow absolve him of his offense, and he might not be executed.

But Thomas Moore turned to her and said,

> Have patience, Margaret. Trouble not thyself. Death comes for us all, even at our birth, death does not stand aside a little. And every day he looks toward us and muses somewhat to himself whether that day or the next he will draw nigh. It is the law of nature, and the will of God.[5]

A few moments later Moore walks up the steps to the executioners platform, and then turns to the headsman and says: "Friend, be not afraid of your office. You send me to God."[6]

What a faith to have in the face of death. Let's voice the prayer of Jesus on our lips to begin and close each day. May we as Christians also be able to express this prayer at the time we face our own death: "Father, into your hands I commit my spirit." May it be true for you and for me.

---

4   Harold S. Kushner, *The Lord Is My Shepherd: Healing Wisdom of the Twenty-Third Psalm* (New York: Alfred A. Knopf, 2003), 109-110.
5   Robert Bolt, *A Man for All Seasons* (New York: Vintage Books, 1962), 93-94
6   *Ibid.*

ALSO BY THE AUTHOR

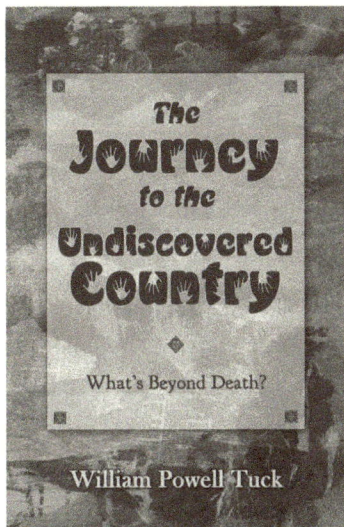

The
Journey
to the
Undiscovered
Country

What's Beyond Death?

William Powell Tuck

With a cautious and pastoral approach, Bill Tuck helps us navigate our way through the questions posed by life and death.

Robert D. Cornwall, PhD
Pastor

This is a serious book about a subject we focus on all too seldom these days — the power and the meaning of the Cross of Christ. I'm glad to say it warmed my heart. I think it will warm yours as well.

John Killinger
Professor, pastor, and author of 50 books, including *The Changing Shape of Our Salvation*

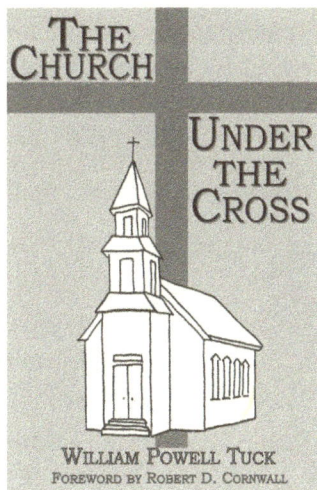

THE CHURCH

UNDER THE CROSS

WILLIAM POWELL TUCK
FOREWORD BY ROBERT D. CORNWALL

MORE FROM ENERGION PUBLICATIONS

Personal Study

Finding My Way in Christianity	Herold Weiss	$16.99
Holy Smoke! Unholy Fire	Bob McKibben	$14.99
The Jesus Paradigm	David Alan Black	$17.99
When People Speak for God	Henry Neufeld	$17.99
The Sacred Journey	Chris Surber	$11.99

Christian Living

Faith in the Public Square	Robert D. Cornwall	$16.99
Grief: Finding the Candle of Light	Jody Neufeld	$8.99
Crossing the Street	Robert LaRochelle	$16.99

Bible Study

Learning and Living Scripture	Lentz/Neufeld	$12.99
From Inspiration to Understanding	Edward W. H. Vick	$24.99
Luke: A Participatory Study Guide	Geoffrey Lentz	$8.99
Philippians: A Participatory Study Guide	Bruce Epperly	$9.99
Ephesians: A Participatory Study Guide	Robert D. Cornwall	$9.99

Theology

Creation in Scripture	Herold Weiss	$12.99
Creation: the Christian Doctrine	Edward W. H. Vick	$12.99
The Politics of Witness	Allan R. Bevere	$9.99
Ultimate Allegiance	Robert D. Cornwall	$9.99
History and Christian Faith	Edward W. H. Vick	$9.99
The Church Under the Cross	William Powell Tuck	$11.99
The Journey to the Undiscovered Country	William Powell Tuck	$9.99
Eschatology: A Participatory Study Guide	Edward W. H. Vick	$9.99

Ministry

Clergy Table Talk	Kent Ira Groff	$9.99
Out of This World	Darren McClellan	$24.99

Generous Quantity Discounts Available
Dealer Inquiries Welcome
Energion Publications — P.O. Box 841
Gonzalez, FL_ 32560
Website: http://energionpubs.com
Phone: (850) 525-3916